This book may be

# COOK
## and the
# Opening of the Pacific

by

JAMES A. WILLIAMSON

NEW YORK
THE MACMILLAN COMPANY
1948

PRINTED IN GREAT BRITAIN

CAPTAIN COOK
The Greenwich Portrait

# Teach Yourself History

VOLUMES READY OR IN PREPARATION

The Use of History, by A. L. Rowse
Pericles and Athens, by A. R. Burn
Alexander the Great and the Hellenistic Empire, by A. R. Burn
Julius Cæsar and the Fall of the Roman Republic,
   by M. I. Henderson
Augustus and the Roman Empire, by M. P. Charlesworth
Constantine and the Conversion of Europe, by A. H. M. Jones
Innocent III and the Mediæval Papacy,
   by A. Hamilton Thompson
Marco Polo and the Discovery of China, by G. F. Hudson
John Wycliffe and the Lollards, by K. B. McFarlane
Henry V and the Invasion of France, by E. F. Jacob
Joan of Arc and the Recovery of France, by Alice Buchan
Erasmus and the Renaissance, by Margaret Mann Phillips
Cranmer and the English Reformation, by F. E. Hutchinson
Raleigh and the British Empire, by D. B. Quinn
Queen Elizabeth and Her Age, by A. L. Rowse
Cromwell and the Puritan Revolution, by Mary Coate
Milton and the English Mind, by F. E. Hutchinson
Gustavus Adolphus and the Thirty Years' War, by Raymond Carr
Richelieu and the French Monarchy, by C. V. Wedgwood
Louis XIV and the Greatness of France, by Maurice Ashley
Peter the Great and the Russian Empire, by B. H. Sumner
Wesley and the Methodist Movement, by Norman Sykes
Chatham and the British Empire, by Sir Charles Grant Robertson
Catherine the Great and the Expansion of Russia,
   by Gladys Scott Thomson
Warren Hastings and British India, by Penderel Moon
Bolívar and the Independence of Spanish America, by J. B. Trend
Jefferson and American Democracy, by Max Beloff
Pushkin and Russian Literature, by Janko Lavrin
Livingstone and Central Africa, by Jack Simmons
Abraham Lincoln and the United States, by K. C. Wheare
Marx, Proudhon and European Socialism, by J. Hampden Jackson
Bismarck and the German Empire, by Con O'Neill
Gladstone and Modern Liberalism, by J. L. Hammond
Parnell and the Irish Nation, by Nicholas Mansergh
Clemenceau and the Third Republic, by J. Hampden Jackson
Woodrow Wilson and American Liberalism, by E. M. Hugh-Jones
Venizelos and Modern Greece, by J. Mavrogordato
Lenin and the Russian Revolution, by Christopher Hill
Botha, Smuts and South Africa, by Basil Williams

# COOK

### and the

# Opening of the Pacific

is one of the volumes
in the
### TEACH YOURSELF HISTORY
### LIBRARY

*Edited by* A. L. ROWSE

# A General Introduction to the Series

THIS series has been undertaken in the conviction that there can be no subject of study more important than history. Great as have been the conquests of natural science in our time —such that many think of ours as a scientific age *par excellence*—it is even more urgent and necessary that advances should be made in the social sciences, if we are to gain control of the forces of nature loosed upon us. The bed out of which all the social sciences spring is history; there they find, in greater or lesser degree, subject-matter and material, verification or contradiction.

There is no end to what we can learn from history, if only we would, for it is coterminous with life. Its special field is the life of man in society, and at every point we can learn vicariously from the experience of others before us in history.

To take one point only—the understanding of politics: how can we hope to understand the world of affairs around us if we do not know how it came to be what it is? How to understand Germany, or Soviet Russia, or the United States —or ourselves, without knowing something of their history?

There is no subject that is more useful, or indeed indispensable.

Some evidence of the growing awareness of this may be seen in the immense increase in the interest of the reading public in history, and the much larger place the subject has come to take in education in our time.

This series has been planned to meet the needs and demands of a very wide public and of education—they are indeed the same. I am convinced that the most congenial, as well as the most concrete and practical, approach to history is the biographical, through the lives of the great men whose actions have been so much part of history, and whose careers in turn have been so moulded and formed by events.

The key idea of this series, and what distinguishes it from any other that has appeared, is the intention by way of a biography of a great man to open up a significant historical theme; for example, Cromwell and the Puritan Revolution, or Lenin and the Russian Revolution.

My hope is, in the end, as the series fills out and completes itself, by a sufficient number of biographies to cover whole periods and subjects in that way. To give you the history of the United States, for example, or the British Empire or France, *via* a number of biographies of their leading historical figures.

That should be something new, as well as convenient and practical, in education.

# GENERAL INTRODUCTION

I need hardly say that I am a strong believer in people with good academic standards writing once more for the general reading public, and of the public being given the best that the universities can provide. From this point of view this series is intended to bring the university into the homes of the people.

A. L. Rowse.

All Souls College,
    Oxford.

# Contents

# Illustrations

# List of Maps

# Preface

ALTHOUGH it contains a short biographical chapter, this book is not mainly a life of Cook but a passage of history in which Cook played the greatest part. The story begins before his time and ends after it. Yet his own work was so outstanding and his personality of such commanding interest that it is inevitable to make him the central figure of the process. The reader will therefore find changes of scale and proportion as the narrative proceeds. There is first an outline of the history of the Pacific before Cook, then a more detailed relation of Cook's achievements, filling the major part of the book, and finally a sketch of the century after him, which saw the opening of the coasts and islands of the Pacific to the enterprise of all the world.

# Acknowledgments

THE Author and Publishers wish to express their grateful thanks for permission to reproduce the Frontispiece portrait of Captain Cook, by Nathanial Dance, by kind permission of the Trustees of the National Maritime Museum; and for the illustration of the model of Captain Cook's *Endeavour Bark*, by courtesy of the Director of the Science Museum, South Kensington, and of C. W. Whitaker, Esq.

*Chapter One*

# The Problems of the Pacific

TWENTY-FIVE centuries ago the geographers of the ancient world had concluded that the earth is not flat but a sphere. This knowledge passed through the Roman Empire to the Christendom of the Middle Ages that followed it, and so in unbroken descent to modern times. The classical geography evolved also the scheme of climates with which we are familiar, the equatorial torrid belt, two temperate zones, and the two frigid polar caps. There were indeed a few mediæval writers who contended vigorously and sometimes abusively that the earth was flat. But even in the darkest times that was the opinion of a minority, and it is safe to say that the spherical earth has always been the established European conception.

Granted the spherical earth and the existence of a south temperate zone beyond the tropics, the conclusion followed that in the southern half of the globe there might be lands like those known to Europeans in the north. In the north were the three continents of Europe, Asia, and Africa, the last unknown south of Egypt and Morocco. The temperate regions of this land-mass harboured many peoples, thinning out into the cold of the Arctic and the heat of the tropics. It was known that Asia had a southern coast and that an ocean stretched thence towards the equator. Some thought that this southern ocean likewise bounded Africa and gave it a coast not far south of Egypt and the Sahara desert; others held that Africa stretched away beyond the equator as a parched and burning land. A further main belief was common, that beyond the southern ocean which somewhere limited Africa and Asia there was an unknown southern continent, *Terra Australis Incognita*, forming a necessary balance to the lands of the northern hemisphere.

So presented, *Terra Australis* might seem exciting, a goal to inspire a quest. But another geographical conception destroyed much of its interest and condemned it to remain for ever unknown. This was the doctrine that the earth's temperate regions were alone inhabitable by man, and that he was unable to endure the cold of the north or the heat of the torrid zone. No man, by this teaching, could pass the equator. And so, if there were a southern continent, it could never be discovered. Imagination might play with nations and kingdoms of antipodean men, but it could never be more than play. Indeed, to churchmen it was speculation with a seed of heresy, for scripture taught that all men were the sons of Adam, and no son of Adam could ever have passed to the south. The Church therefore discouraged belief in the antipodes, the people of the south. But in so teaching, it did not by any means assert that the earth was flat, as it has often been accused of doing.

As the dark centuries after the decline of Rome gave way to the later Middle Ages with their increasing enterprise and zest for knowledge, Europeans began to travel more widely and to make contacts with Africans and Asiatics. Information gradually spread to cast doubt on the old dogma of the impassability of the tropics. In the fourteenth century writers were claiming that men might go "under" the globe to its southern parts. In the fifteenth century men were doing it. The Portuguese sailed along the West African coast until they passed the equator and returned unscathed; and when Vasco da Gama made his Indian voyage round southern Africa in 1497–9 he achieved a navigation through part of the southern ocean.

So far we have considered the southern ocean and the supposed southern continent as encircling the whole globe south of the equator. This southern ocean is not the same thing as the Pacific, although nearly half of it coincides with the South Pacific. The Pacific itself during all those centuries was an impossible conception, for it means the ocean between America and Asia; and until the end of the fifteenth century there was no America. The world north of the equator was believed to hold only the three adjacent

3

continents, Europe, Asia, and Africa; and, by consequence, the sea that washed the western shores of Europe washed also the eastern shores of Asia. From this it was easily deduced that the directest way to eastern Asia was to sail west from Europe. It was the plan upon which Columbus acted, but it had been a fancy of learned men since the days of the Roman Empire.

The Spanish sovereigns made Columbus Admiral of the Ocean Sea, his jurisdiction extending from Castile to Cathay. But when the western discovery turned out to be a new and unsuspected continent, the Ocean Sea was divided into two oceans, the Atlantic between Europe and America, and another between America and Asia. The discovery of America and the recognition of the Pacific are two aspects of the same fact. Some years elapsed before the new ocean was named. The first European to see it from the American side was the Spaniard Balboa, who crossed the isthmus of Panama in 1513 and struck the boundless waters with his sword, claiming them as the dominion of Spain. Balboa called his discovery the South Sea. Seven years later Magellan the Portuguese, sailing in the service of Spain, passed through the straits named after him and crossed the ocean to the islands of eastern Asia. He named the ocean the Pacific. The two names continued in use for the best part of four centuries, for most of which time the South Sea was the more popular of the

4

two. But in our own time it has gone completely out of fashion, and the Pacific Ocean is the unchallenged designation.

With Magellan's achievement in the early sixteenth century the Pacific takes shape. In its northern half it is the ocean between America and Asia, and chiefly interesting on that account, as part of a western highway from Europe to the Far East. In its southern half it comprises a great part of the southern ocean of antiquity, and serves as the chief location of those ancient fantasies of *Terra Australis* and the antipodes, fantasies soon to be transformed into projects of vigorous enterprise. For nearly three centuries—from the early sixteenth to the late eighteenth—Pacific exploration falls into these two categories: the development of the highway and the revelation of unknown lands. In a long process Spaniards, Portuguese, Englishmen, Dutchmen, and Frenchmen all bore arduous part. But the field was vast and progress slow. After two hundred and fifty years the solved problems of the Pacific were little as compared with the unsolved. And then came a great practical genius, James Cook, who cleared up all the major uncertainties in ten years of effort, and left little but details to be rounded off by his successors. Although Cook was the climax of Pacific enterprise, he was not its beginner. To make clear what he did, it will be necessary to review briefly the earlier achievements.

The papal bulls of 1493, occasioned by the first western discoveries of Columbus, established the principle that from a dividing meridian passing down the middle of the Atlantic the Portuguese should enjoy the monopoly of empire-building eastwards, and the Spaniards westwards. With success their pioneers would of course meet on the other side of the world, but the problem of defining the meridian opposite to that of 1493 was left until the occasion should arise. The Portuguese reached India in 1498, and in the following years they rapidly seized the controlling seaports of the Indian Ocean. In 1511 they captured Malacca and, once through its straits, were in the waters of the western Pacific. They were intent upon the valuable trade of eastern Asia and its archipelago of spice-bearing islands, and they made no attempt to thrust across the Pacific as the Spaniards were soon to do from the opposite side. The Portuguese entered the Moluccas, the most valuable spice islands, in 1512, having coasted the north side of Java to reach them. Borneo and Celebes, on the way to the Moluccas, quickly became known, and also the chain of small islands running eastwards from Java to Timor. In 1526-7 a new eastward push revealed the north coast of New Guinea. In the meantime the Portuguese had turned northwards and one of their expeditions had reached China in 1516. In 1542 they made their first contact with Japan. The

Portuguese were concerned only with the Asiatic side of the Pacific, and their approach to it was always by the Cape of Good Hope and the Indian Ocean. Somewhere in or east of their spice islands ran the meridian which was the opposite number of that dividing the Spanish and Portuguese spheres in the Atlantic. No one could say precisely where it was owing to the inadequacy of the means of determining longitude. But on general grounds it was evident that the vast extent of the Pacific was a Spanish claim. Portugal never showed any interest in it as a highway from Europe. Whether she was equally indifferent to the possibility of *Terra Australis Incognita* is a difficult question to which no certain answer can be given.

There is no written record that any early Portuguese navigator went to the south of the Java–Timor chain of islands or along the south coast of New Guinea. But there does exist a series of world-maps made by French cartographers in the period 1530–50; and these maps show a great land roughly in the position now known to be occupied by Australia and with a coastline not inconsistent with some actual knowledge of the Australian coast. There is no possibility that this represents a French discovery, but there is a possibility that the Portuguese coasted a considerable part of Australia before 1530 and that one of their charts came into the hands of a French geographer.

The controversy is between those who deny the discovery and hold that the maps represent mere guesswork, which they have to admit is uncannily near the truth; and those who are convinced that there must have been a discovery, but have to find reasons why it should have been kept secret and expunged from all the written records of the Portuguese Indies. No conclusive answer has yet been given, and none can truly say whether Australia was first discovered by the Portuguese in the sixteenth century or by the Dutch in the seventeenth.

Meanwhile the Pacific as a highway to Asia was exercising the Spaniards and the English. The numerous attempts to find the North West Passage round the northern shores of America represent one line of approach to the linking of Atlantic and Pacific. The North West Passage was never accomplished, and so the early voyages in search of it never became Pacific voyages. But hope remained bright in the sixteenth and seventeenth centuries and was not dead in the eighteenth. It was destined to provide the main motive of Cook's last expedition. Magellan's undertaking was to find the corresponding South West Passage round the end of South America. He discovered the straits between the continent and Tierra del Fuego. Magellan himself did not think that Tierra del Fuego was of any great size and correctly believed that the main ocean lay not far away to the southward of the strait he was traversing. But the academic geographers, their minds full of the great southern continent, made Tierra del Fuego a part of it, and drew the Straits of Magellan as the single narrow waterway between two vast land-masses, the one extending north to the tropics, the other south to the pole. Thus Tierra del Fuego, in reality a smallish island, was accepted as the first-seen instalment of the promised *Terra Australis Incognita*. The strait was only a step to Magellan's main purpose, which was to lead a Spanish expedition to the Spice Islands by the western route that lay all in the waters assigned to the Spanish Crown by the papal bulls. The uncertainty of longitude provided the excuse for this proceeding. It was really a trespass on the Portuguese, for modern determination of longitudes has shown that the Moluccas were within their hemisphere as the world was partitioned by the bulls. But at the time neither they nor the intruders could be positive on the point. Magellan crossed the Pacific in the trade-wind belt of the tropics, finding the ocean infinitely wider than had been expected. He discovered the Philippine Islands and was there killed in battle with the natives. The expedition then went south to the Moluccas, where the Portuguese were already collecting spices. Two ships now survived of Magellan's original five. One of them attempted to sail back to America, but was baffled by the prevailing winds and ultimately

9

surrendered to the Portuguese in the islands. The last ship, the *Victoria*, under the command of Sebastian del Cano, passed westwards out of the archipelago, crossed the Indian Ocean, rounded the Cape, and reached Spain in 1522 after making the first circumnavigation of the globe.

The Pacific had been crossed, but its size was terrifying to imaginations accustomed to regard the Atlantic as the limit of vastness. With the slow ships, the perishable gear, and the primitive victualling of those days it was just possible, and no more, to struggle across in Magellan's track at the price of a high percentage of deaths from scurvy. But this entailed only a partial establishment of the highway, since return by the same track proved to be impossible. The Spaniards sent out other expeditions after the *Victoria's* return. Of their ships which reached the Spice Islands not one came back, and the few surviving men came home to Europe as passengers or prisoners with the Portuguese sailing through the Indian Ocean. These Spanish voyages provide a possible explanation of Portuguese silence on the discovery—if it was made—of Australia. The Australian coasts, as we know, can have offered no trade of any value, and the Portuguese had too few ships and men for their main purpose of dominating the spice trade. They had therefore no incentive to further the Australian discovery on their own account. But the Australian continent might have attracted Spanish empire-builders as the American had done, and a Spanish colony would have provided shipping debilitated by the Pacific crossing with a base for refreshment and refit before proceeding to operations in the spice archipelago. It may therefore have been made a Portuguese policy to suppress all knowledge of Australia, as they had previously attempted to conceal information about West Africa from the same fear of aiding intruders. "Security silence" is the current phrase for it.

Disappointed by the failure to open a both-way track across the Pacific, the Emperor Charles V (King of Spain) sold his claim on the Moluccas to the Portuguese, and thenceforward left them undisturbed in the spice trade. Spain, however, retained her claim to Magellan's discovery of the Philippines, which were regarded as a valuable advanced base for trade with China. Their exploitation remained dormant until 1564, when a colonizing expedition crossed the Pacific from Mexico and took what proved to be permanent possession. It was of course a gamble on the opening of a return route. To sail back against the north-east trade wind had been proved impossible. But in 1565 Andres de Urdaneta, a navigator in the expedition, took a cast northwards from the Philippines until he came to a latitude where westerly winds prevailed, and these brought him back to California and so, by coasting south, to Mexico. For the first time the Pacific had been re-crossed. The passage could be made only by getting clear of the Philippines at a limited season of the year, and then it took from four to six months to reach America. But the Spaniards found it worth while, and Manila became an entrepôt which collected gold, silks, lacquerware, and porcelain from Chinese merchants in exchange for the silver of Mexico.

Magellan's voyage and the Spanish interest in the Pacific fired the imagination of Robert Thorne, an English merchant doing business in Seville. After writing a preliminary explanation of his ideas in 1527 to the English ambassador then in Spain, Thorne collaborated in 1530 with another merchant, Roger Barlow, to produce an address to Henry VIII entitled *The Declaration of the Indies*. The "Indies" which they had in mind were the vast and wealthy lands thought to be awaiting discovery in the Pacific. Although Thorne nowhere uses the name, he was intent on *Terra Australis Incognita* and its adjacent islands. As the Spaniards were creating an empire in America and the Portuguese in Asia, so he believed that these southern lands would fall to the English if the King would rise to his destiny. Thorne's geography was nourished on the study of the globe rather than of the trouble-saving but misleading flat maps which too often satisfy us in these days. The globe showed him that the shortest way from England to the equatorial Pacific was due north over the Pole and then

straight on south by the opposite meridian. S
would a ship come to those unknown Indies by a
very much shorter passage than the Portuguese
could make round their Cape of Good Hope or
the Spaniards through their Straits of Magellan.
There were two large assumptions in this, that
the ship would not be stopped by arctic ice, and
that there was a strait between America and
Asia to allow access to the Pacific from the north.
Optimism about the ice was unjustified, but the
strait was a guess that turned out to be correct.
The sixteenth century called it the Straits of
Anian, but no one saw it then, and in the
eighteenth century it was named Bering Strait
from its discoverer.

No action was taken on Thorne's project in
his own lifetime, but his *Declaration*, although it
remained unprinted for nearly sixty years, was
known to those who studied the advancement of
discovery. It helped to build up that extra-
ordinary and detailed belief in *Terra Australis
Incognita*, which became more powerful in the
sixteenth century than ever before, and dominated
southern exploration until the time of Captain
Cook. The conception was reinforced by Magellan's report of Tierra del Fuego to the south of
his straits and by the French maps, already
referred to, depicting a great land-mass south of
the Portuguese Indies. A generation of theoretical
geographers linked these two by drawing a long
continental coast running diagonally across the

acific from the Straits of Magellan in 54° S. to a locality south of Java in 15° S. This was the maximum scope attained by *Terra Australis* so far as it concerned the Pacific. The great continent was also considered as bounding the South Atlantic and Indian Oceans. But there it was thought to lie farther to the southward and to be less generally attractive. Only in its Pacific area did it comprise all the temperate latitudes and extend well into the tropics. A matter of doubt was the relation of New Guinea to the main continent. No discovery of the south coast of New Guinea was on record, and some, perhaps the majority, believed that it had no south coast; in other words, that it was joined to the continent. But the best authorities held the point to be unsettled, and some depicted New Guinea as an island. The uncertainty persisted for two centuries until it was solved by Cook.

By 1570 the above conception of the southern continent had been fully elaborated. In that year it was so depicted by the Flemish geographer Abraham Ortelius in his published atlas, which became a standard authority in Europe. From various sources economic information was added to the geographical outline. It was a common belief in the sixteenth century that gold, silver, and precious stones were more likely to be found in the tropics than in other regions, and that gold in particular was somehow engendered by the heat of the sun. The tropical extension of

14

*Terra Australis* was therefore regarded as likely to produce mineral wealth. Thorne's *Declaration* spoke of "lands and islands situated between the tropics and under the equinoctial [the equator] . . . the richest lands and islands of the world, of gold, precious stones, balms, spices and other things that we here esteem most." Nearly fifty years later an Elizabethan memorial on the same region declared: "We are assured to expect gold, silver, pearls, rich grain, and such most precious merchandise, besides countries of most excellent temperature to be inhabited." The biblical record of King Solomon's fleets and the riches they brought from the land of Ophir was interpreted as referring to *Terra Australis* and helped to build up the general expectations of advantage. More powerful still was the effect of certain passages in the *Travels* of Marco Polo, the Venetian who had made his way all over central and southern Asia in the thirteenth century. Marco Polo made some statements about the Malay peninsula and the adjacent islands, but these were garbled by transcribers of his manuscript and made to refer to great lands as yet undiscovered by Europeans, regions of the southern continent rich in gold, spices, and aromatic drugs. Marco's names for these lands, Locach, Pentam, Malaiur, were inscribed by Ortelius on his *Terra Australis*, with added phrases about the gold and the perfumes. Altogether *Terra Australis Incognita* had become a glittering prize by the second half

15

of the sixteenth century, a continent with all the wealth of America, fringed by islands comparable to the West Indies, awaiting a new Columbus to lead a new band of conquering adventurers to its exploitation. Was the new Columbus to be a Spaniard or an Englishman? The choice seemed to lie between these two.

Spain tried first in the persons of Alvaro de Mendaña and Pedro Sarmiento de Gamboa, who fitted out two ships in Peru in 1567. Fortified by Indian stories of an Inca prince who had found land in the west, they expected to reach the southern continent in its tropical extension only 600 leagues from the South American coast. This was much nearer than Ortelius or other contemporary geographers would have put it. Mendaña and Sarmiento sailed in the required latitude and far beyond the distance at which they had hoped to find the land. Nothing was seen, and they altered course a little northwards and still pushed into the west. At length, after a voyage through 120 degrees of longitude close to the equator, very nearly one-third of the earth's circumference, they discovered a group of large islands between 5° and 10° S. and gave them names, Isabella, Guadalcanal, Malaita, San Christoval, which are still in use. The Spaniards spent six months of 1568 in exploring the group, alternately on friendly and fighting terms with the very spirited inhabitants. Mendaña tried to get geographical information in

16

spite of the language barrier, and believed that the islanders were telling him of a continent and a civilized people farther on. No gold was found, but again optimism discerned signs of its presence, and the whole discovery seemed most promising. The way back was by Urdaneta's great semicircle round the northern Pacific, which brought the expedition to California and Mexico, and then after a lengthy coasting at last to Peru. In the Mexican seaports Mendaña and his crew related their adventures, and it was placed on record that he had discovered the islands of King Solomon. Whether he made that claim is not clear, but it was current in Mexico immediately upon his return, and the discovery has been known as the Solomon Islands ever since.

Mendaña was anxious to exploit his discovery, but in fact nothing followed. Political jealousies and a change of viceroy in Peru prevented immediate action, and he had to go to Spain to seek support. Even when he had it, colonial obstructionists thwarted him, and the years slipped by until the situation was altered by the entry of the English into the Pacific. In sum it was nearly thirty years before Mendaña, his driving power weakened by long frustration, was able to sail again on the quest of his youth.

Meanwhile the English were at work. English merchants in Mexico heard the tale of the Solomon Islands and the continent beyond. Soon the news came to England, where it gave confirmation to the geographers' assertion of *Terra Australis* and its great continental coast from Tierra del Fuego to the Portuguese Indies so alluringly drawn in the atlas of Ortelius. A syndicate of Devon magnates and shipowners under Sir Richard Grenville obtained a preliminary sanction from the Queen to exploit the Pacific. They intended primarily to explore and colonize *Terra Australis* and trade in its commodities. But the highway was also in their plans. Their shipping could go on across the Pacific to trade with eastern Asia. It could also, at the proper season of the year, seek return to England by the North West Passage, approached from the Pacific side. In short, this plan of empire-building combined all the possibilities, from those of Robert Thorne fifty years before to those of Martin Frobisher, who was even then working from the Atlantic to open the North West Passage. But in one respect the Devon projectors differed from both Thorne and Frobisher. They were firm that the first approach to the scene of action should be through the Straits of Magellan. They insisted that the principal scene of operations would be the great continent south of the equator—"having the pole antarctic elevate," as they put it—and that even the trade with Asia would be only a sideshow. After favouring the scheme, Elizabeth changed her mind in 1574 and withdrew her consent; and Grenville never led the expedition into the South Sea. The Queen's reason can only be inferred, but there is not much doubt of it. In 1573–4 she was working to patch up the English differences with Spain and secure a permanent peace. Grenville in the Pacific would be very near the golden coast of Peru, whence Spain shipped her South American treasure. If he should add treasure-raiding to discovery, as most likely he would, being that sort of man, great diplomatic plans would be imperilled. So the project was suspended.

It was not suspended for long. In 1577 it came forward again, this time as a semi-official undertaking patronized by ministers of the Crown and supported by officials of the Admiralty. For reasons unexplained, Grenville had withdrawn from the leadership, and Francis Drake was in his place. The Queen was now complaisant. She was no longer timorous about treasure-raiding, but was even ready to connive at it. Relations with Spain had deteriorated, and the attempt at good friendship had broken down.

Drake sailed for the Pacific at the close of 1577. It was given out that he was bound for Alexandria, and so his sailors were led to believe. It is now known that the promoters of the voyage had for their objective the plan of empire-building in *Terra Australis*. It is also well known that nothing of the sort was in fact attempted. Drake and the Queen and her Secretary Walsingham had a private plan which overrode the other. Drake passed through the Straits of Magellan and then sought, not *Terra Australis* to the north-westward, but Chile and Peru to the northward. On those coasts he ballasted his *Golden Hind* with treasure, which he took with the utmost ease and scarcely any fighting. Spain had been caught with her South Sea interests undefended. Drake, however, had made an involuntary contribution to discovery. On issuing from the Straits of Magellan he had been driven south by storms and had found only the open ocean in a region that should by theory have been continental land. He had been round the western side of Tierra del Fuego to the neighbourhood of Cape Horn—which he may have seen, although the fact is not established—and he believed that the Atlantic and Pacific here met and merged so that one could sail from the one into the other without using the Straits. Drake did not publish his discovery, although it became well known to initiated seamen, both English and Dutch. But so conservative was seafaring mankind that forty years elapsed before anyone attempted to sail round Cape Horn. Drake had knocked the first hole in that edifice of theory the southern continent; but belief was not easily shattered, and in other directions the edifice continued to grow.

After finishing his treasure-raid on the Peruvian coast, Drake crossed the equator northwards with two alternatives in mind, to return to

England through the North West Passage, or to cross the Pacific to Asia and thence sail home round the Cape of Good Hope. According to a theory almost as firmly held as that of *Terra Australis*, the North West Passage opened from the Atlantic, where Frobisher had been operating, in a latitude of about 60–65 degrees, but slanted south-westwards and debouched into the Pacific in about 40 degrees. Drake went considerably higher than this without finding any channel through the Californian coast. He was then obliged to stop for a month to refit the ship in an unidentified Californian harbour, after which the season of the year (1579) was too late for any further attempt to use the Passage. He therefore crossed the Pacific in the trade-wind latitudes, visited the Moluccas, and completed the circumnavigation of the world by way of the Indian Ocean and the Cape. Drake's *Golden Hind* was the first English vessel to thread the Straits and capture treasure on the Peruvian coast, to visit California and cross the Pacific, to lade spices in the Moluccas, and to sail round the Cape of Good Hope.

Spain had felt so secure on her Pacific treasure coast that she had not armed a ship or fortified a seaport on its whole extent. Drake's success in that part of his undertaking was therefore swift and sweeping. Other captains sought to follow his example and had to fight harder. Thomas Cavendish made a successful circumnavigation in

1586–8. He lost many men for little gain on the South American coast and found his booty farther north when he intercepted a galleon bound for Mexico from Manila. On a second voyage he failed to get through the Straits and died at sea. The Straits of Magellan foiled two or three other expeditions, and then Richard Hawkins got through in 1593–4. He, like Cavendish, had no thoughts of *Terra Australis* (so completely had Drake's action changed the fashion in South Sea projecting), but designed to raid the treasure coast and then proceed to eastern Asia to make arrangements for the opening of a regular English trade. But Spain had now learnt her lesson and had a powerful squadron on the west coast. Hawkins was caught and forced to surrender after a heroic three days' fight; and his was the last English ship to enter the Pacific for many a year to come.

During all this time the English intrusion had been holding back Mendaña, who pleaded in vain to be allowed to resume his discoveries. Of what use, it was answered, would it be to make discoveries which the English would promptly utilize? The defeat of Hawkins in 1594 showed that the English menace could be mastered, and Spanish confidence was so far restored that Mendaña was permitted to proceed.

He sailed with four ships from Callao in 1595, intending to colonize the Solomon Islands and discover the southern continent thought to lie not far beyond. His most notable subordinate was Pedro Fernandez de Quiros, a Portuguese who served as chief pilot. Mendaña himself was deeply religious and benevolently disposed towards the natives of the South Sea Islands, regarding the undertaking primarily as one for saving souls rather than for making fortunes. Quiros fully shared these views, and it was a tragedy for both men that they lacked the power to control their unruly followers, who wantonly committed atrocious actions and made missionary work impossible. Although Mendaña had made full and accurate descriptions of the islands he had seen nearly thirty years before, he was very hazy about their position and greatly under-estimated their distance from Peru. He was in fact unable to find them, and they were destined never to be seen again by any European until the latter half of the eighteenth century. What he did do was to discover the attractive islands in 10° S., which he called the Marquesas in compliment to the Marquis de Cañete, the Vice-roy of Peru. These were about half way to the true position of the Solomons, but already Mendaña felt that he was almost there. After a prolonged further passage, with increasing dis-content and insubordination, he reached a large island which he was sure was one of the Solomons; but on closer view he had to admit that the natives were of a different race. Here, however, he decided to found the colony, and here he died of fever and vexation in the attempt to do so. For the crews showed no disposition to work and would not behave decently to the natives; and after two months it was obvious that there could be no success. Quiros, succeeding to the command, reluctantly abandoned the island, which had been named Santa Cruz and lies about 200 miles east of the nearest Solomons. He led the survivors on a course north-westwards to the Philippines, and at Manila the few who were left recovered their health and ultimately worked their ship back to America.

Quiros was thirty at the time of this adventure, and at the age of forty he was able to try again. The ten years' interval was accounted for by the official postponement and obstruction that clogged all Spanish action. During the interval his character developed. He became a saint and a mystic and at the same time more incapable than ever of controlling a ship's crew and imposing his will on the conduct of an expedition. His whole mind was filled with the idea of finding the great continent and saving the souls of its inhabitants, and he had little thought to spare for the supervision of details and the maintenance of discipline. His mental condition may be gauged from the occasion on which he refused to give the helmsmen a course, saying that the ships might go where they would and God would guide them right.

He sailed from Peru at the close of 1605 with

Luis Vaez de Torres, another Portuguese, in command of his second ship. Next year, after the usual long passage and sighting of minor islands, the expedition came to the larger units of the New Hebrides, the greatest of which Quiros mistook for continental land. He named it Austrialia del Espiritu Santo. There followed a profusion of religious ceremonies, pageants, the creation of an Order of Knights of the Holy Ghost of which every ruffian in the crew became a member, the choice of the site for a City of New Jerusalem, and then a sudden decision to call everything off and sail elsewhere. All hands embarked, and the ships put to sea. Quiros then made another decision, to return and build a fort on the shore of the bay he had just abandoned. That was the end of him as a commander. Torres complied with the order and brought his ship to anchor in the bay, but the ship of Quiros was apparently unable to beat in against the offshore breeze. Finally she disappeared and was seen no more. Her crew had deliberately mishandled her in order to part company and give up the voyage: "They did not sail on the proper course, or with good intention," wrote Torres. Although there is no proof of a formal mutiny, Quiros had ceased to exercise command and in due course was carried back to Mexico, whence he travelled to Spain to spend his last years in appeals for a new expedition to be entrusted to him.

Left to himself, Torres proceeded to make the last and in one aspect the most important of the Spanish discoveries. Leaving the New Hebrides he sailed some 400 miles to the south-west in search of the veritable continent. It was about half the distance which would have brought him to the coast of the real Australia had he persisted on the same course. Shortage of victuals made him turn north-westwards for Manila, a passage which would normally have been made along the north side of New Guinea. Torres failed to weather the eastern end of this great land and made his way to the Philippines by coasting its south side. By so doing he proved that it had a south side and was an island. Geographers had hitherto been uncertain on the matter, and some had made New Guinea all one with the theoretical southern continent. Others had tentatively drawn a strait, but had not been positive of its existence. Now Torres had passed through this strait, which is justly named Torres Strait in his memory. It is a curious circumstance that he does not speak of the achievement as an important new discovery, but rather alludes to it as the making of a passage which he already knew to exist. He was a Portuguese. Had he some traditional knowledge of suppressed discoveries of the previous century? On another point we should be clear. Torres was conscious of having coasted southern New Guinea, but not of having sighted an Australian continent to the southward.

His track took him through a maze of shoals, reefs, and low islands, amongst which, if he ever sighted Cape York, the northernmost point of Australia, it probably appeared as only one more island among many. What his voyage proved was not the existence of northern Australia but the insularity of New Guinea.

The discovery did not become part of public knowledge in Torres's own time. On arriving at Manila he wrote an account of it, and this account remained unpublished until the eighteenth century. Diego de Prado, a Spanish officer who sailed with him, also wrote an account which lay still longer in oblivion, for its existence remained unknown until our own times, and it was first published in 1930. Geographers therefore had no more information of the existence of the strait than they had previously possessed, and as time went on opinion hardened against it. When the real Australia came indubitably into view, it was commonly believed to be a land continuous with New Guinea.

Whatever may or may not have occurred previously, the indubitable discovery of the real Australia was by the Dutch. In 1595 their first expedition sailed round the Cape to the East Indies and began the task of ousting the Portuguese from the spice trade. Ten years later they were sufficiently established to begin an investigation of what might lie to the south of New Guinea. In 1605 a small Dutch vessel under Willem

27

Janszoon sailed from Bantam, and early in the next year began to coast the southern shore of New Guinea from its western end, thus tracing it in the opposite direction to that followed by Torres later in the same year. Having arrived at the western entrance to Torres Strait, Janszoon did not enter it, and apparently did not recognize that it was a strait. While not certain on the point, he seems to have thought it likely that the maze of reefs and islands fringed a continuous shore running north and south. He turned south, picked up an unmistakable mainland coast, and followed it into what we now call the Gulf of Carpentaria. By so doing Janszoon became the first commander on record who discovered any part of the true Australia. He did not press southward far enough to reach the end of the Gulf of Carpentaria, and for long it remained uncertain whether this water was a closed gulf or the opening of a strait penetrating right through the continent. The Dutch, then, had discovered Australia but, in spite of the opportunity, they had not discovered Torres Strait; nor did they learn of its discovery when Torres effected it.

Western Australia is not in the Pacific, but its discovery may here be briefly accounted for. From 1616 the Dutch shipping sailing to the East Indies abandoned the Portuguese practice of using the south-west monsoon in the equatorial latitudes of the Indian Ocean. Instead the

Dutch captains kept a more southerly course in latitudes between 30° and 40° S., sailing in the belt of westerly winds until they had reached the proper longitude in which to turn north for the Asiatic islands. By so doing they speedily became acquainted with the West Australian coast. They first sighted it in 1616 and gradually discerned its length and characteristics in the subsequent years. The same process also accounted for the discovery of about half (the western half) of the south coast, while expeditions sent from Batavia learned more about the Gulf of Carpentaria and traced the north-western coast of Australia. The Dutch called the country New Holland and were disappointed with it. Instead of offering the wealth of Marco Polo's Locach or Solomon's Ophir, it appeared to be utterly barren and useless. By 1640 it was generally agreed that the north-western, western, and south-western coasts were those of one land-mass, and that New Guinea comprised not only the land we so describe but also that to the east of the Gulf of Carpentaria, which had not even yet been probed to the end. Should that gulf turn out to be a dividing channel it would have New Holland to the west of it and New Guinea, extending indefinitely southwards, to the east. It must be repeated that this New Guinea conception was held in ignorance of what Torres had done; for Torres had cut the Dutchmen's New Guinea in two.

Besides exploring the Australian approaches to the Pacific, the Dutch did something to increase the area of knowledge in the great ocean itself. Some of the Dutch trading expeditions to the East Indies went by way of the Straits of Magellan and across the Pacific more or less in Magellan's track. These made no discoveries. But in 1615 two Dutch commanders, Willem Schouten and Jacob Le Maire, sailed on an expedition that was novel in method and purpose. The Dutch East India Company had the legal monopoly of voyaging to the Indies either by the Cape of Good Hope or the Straits of Magellan. Schouten and Le Maire were not members of the Company, and they purposed to circumvent the monopoly by ignoring the straits and going round the south of Tierra del Fuego, in the open ocean which Drake had found nearly forty years before. Once in the South Sea, their primary object would be, not trade with the East Indies, but the discovery of *Terra Australis Incognita* and its supposed civilized inhabitants.

They duly accomplished the new passage, sighting and naming Cape Horn in 1616. Before reaching it they passed between Tierra del Fuego and a lofty coast which is now called Staten Island, of no great extent or significance. The explorers, seeing only part of this island, mistook its nature and assumed it to be part of the southern continent. They gave it the name of Staten Land and conceived themselves to have discovered another narrow strait comparable to the Straits of Magellan. This, a new access to the Pacific, was the principal discovery. After making it the expedition crossed the ocean, as so many others had done, in the trade-wind belt, and encountered only islands of minor importance. As it drew near to New Guinea, with the intention of passing on to Batavia, the choice arose of going north or south of the great island. The Dutchmen did not know that Torres had gone south and that a passage existed. They feared that if there were no passage they would be jammed against a coast from which the prevailing wind would not permit withdrawal, and so they chose the known passage north of New Guinea. This reasoning led every subsequent west-bound explorer until Cook to shirk pressing into the area of mystery south of New Guinea, and was the cause why it was left to him, late in the eighteenth century, to be the discoverer of eastern Australia.

In the North Pacific the Dutch of this period made some detailed discoveries on the Japanese coasts, but they did not succeed in determining the general shape and layout of the Japanese archipelago and the islands to the northward. There were persistent rumours, originated by Spaniards who made the northern passage from the Philippines to Mexico, that rich and civilized lands with white inhabitants existed between Japan and North America. The Dutch made some attempts on this problem. They naturally found nothing, but they did not succeed in proving that there was nothing to find.

The period of Dutch exploration in the Pacific culminated and ended with the discoveries of Abel Tasman, with whose name must be coupled that of his chief pilot Frans Visscher. In 1642 Anthony Van Diemen, governor-general of the Dutch Indies, despatched these two on a voyage with the following chief purposes: to traverse the southern Indian Ocean in latitudes higher than 40° S., the usual southern limit of the Indiamen sailing from the Cape to Western Australia; to pass south of Australia itself and to determine whether or not it was connected with the main mass of *Terra Australis Incognita*; if it was not so connected, to see whether there was open water for a passage across the Pacific to Chile in the belt of westerly winds which lay south of the tropical east-wind belt. The long Dutch war of independence against Spain was still unconcluded in the 1640's, and a passage to Chile and Peru through southern latitudes would permit of surprise treasure-raiding impossible by the northern route.

Tasman sailed with two ships from Batavia to Mauritius, a westerly vantage-point from which to plunge south into the high unknown latitudes. Having made his southern progress from Mauritius, he drove eastwards between 40° and 50° S., before the great west winds of that zone, known to later sailors as the roaring forties. No continental land was seen, and *Terra Australis* shrank backwards in its Indian Ocean section. The course took Tasman south of and out of sight of New Holland, but brought him to his first positive discovery farther on, the land now justly called Tasmania, but by him named Van Diemen's Land. He was out to survey broad possibilities, not the minor details. He therefore did not stay to clear up the relationship of his new land with New Holland and New Guinea, but rounded it by the south and sailed on into the open Pacific. By so doing he proved that the continental lands discovered by the Dutch—the true Australia— were not part of the great southern continent extending to the antarctic pole. The first part of the southern route from Java to America had been established. Tasman now tackled the next. He had to find whether a land barrier blocked the way in the latitudes where westerly winds prevailed. If it did, the navigator would be forced northwards into the belt of the south-east trades and his progress would be stopped. Twelve hundred miles' sailing from Tasmania brought Tasman to a coastline running north and south. He named it Staten Land, soon altered to New Zealand, and assumed that it was part of the great southern continent. He found that to the northward it ended in a promontory, which he called Cape Maria Van Diemen, many degrees south of the trade-wind zone. With the academic maps colouring his mind he conceived the continental coast as slanting away south-eastwards to the region of Cape Horn. His own new cape must therefore be the northernmost point of the continent. His own problem was solved: there was a practicable seaway by the south to Chile. Although he had completely mistaken the nature of New Zealand, Tasman was right on the question that mainly exercised him. He returned by the north of New Guinea to Batavia.

Tasman and Visscher had still a task to perform. Was there a channel south of New Guinea? And was the Gulf of Carpentaria the opening of a channel that passed southward right through Australia? In 1644 they sailed to answer these questions. They coasted the south-west of New Guinea until they came to the obstructed entrance of Torres Strait; and, like the previous Dutch explorers, they failed to perceive that it was a strait. The map which they constructed shows New Guinea and Australia as one continuous land. The other question they solved correctly by reaching the extremity of the Gulf of Carpentaria and following its shore round westwards. It was a closed gulf and not an open channel, and New Holland was all one with the alleged New Guinea. This was the last important Dutch exploration. Governor-general Van Diemen died in the following year, and with him the spirit of discovery in governing circles.

## Chapter Two

# From Dampier to Bougainville

AFTER Tasman's voyages there was a halt in Pacific exploration for more than fifty years. The oceanic powers had different reasons for abstention. Portugal, having revolted against Spanish rule, had a long fight for independence, and after achieving it concentrated her imperial interests on Brazil and the remains of her African possessions. In the East she had scarcely any power remaining and made no attempt at revival. Spain was still strong in her American empire, but her statesmen admitted that her days of conquest were ended. She claimed the South Sea as her monopoly but had no desire to reveal any more of its possibilities, for they would certainly be exploited by others. The Dutch, having achieved the monopoly of the Asiatic archipelago and its spice trade, relapsed into the somewhat demoralizing occupation of squeezing the utmost wealth out of the possession, and decided after Van Diemen's death that far-flung new enterprise was neither necessary nor desirable. England and France were hard at work throughout the seventeenth century in founding their colonial empires in America and the West Indies and in

taking the preliminary steps to empire in India.
So the unknown Pacific faded out of calculation,
and the known Pacific shrank to two thinly used
traffic lanes, the outward and homeward tracks
between Mexico and the Philippines. No other
ships than the "Manila galleons" on this service
crossed the Pacific. Apart from the coasting
traffic of Chile and Peru, the waters south of the
equator were cleft by not a single European keel,
and the islanders who had seen the sails of
Mendaña and Tasman, and had felt the sting
of the white man's shot, forgot the experience
and returned to the carefree life of Nature's
children in Nature's happiest playground.

The writings of William Dampier, coupled
with a major breakdown in Europe's state system,
revived the European interest in the Pacific.
We may take the political breakdown first. It
was the extinction of the Spanish royal line of
the Hapsburg family, which had built up the
Spanish Empire, and the appearance of a French
candidate with a colourable claim to the inherit-
ance. Spain under the Hapsburgs had become
satiated and easy-going, and had settled down
to rule her great American empire on conservative lines without new enterprise or expansion.
Spaniards also, even in their days of energy, had
been a military nation and had never shown any
genius for the creation and use of sea power.
But the potentialities of the Spanish western
empire were enormous, and in the hands of

vigorous Frenchmen they might be realized.
France in control of most of South America, of
the greatest islands in the West Indies, of all
Central America, and of the greater part of
North America, would not let things sleep. She
would grow supreme in oceanic trade and sea
power. She would reach out over the Pacific,
perhaps find and dominate the southern continent, certainly impinge upon eastern Asia and
its archipelago, and then be able to reinforce
her existing outposts in India. This was the
prospect which perturbed English and Dutch
statesmen as the seventeenth century drew to
its close. The last Spanish Hapsburg, an invalid
extremely tenacious of life, was dying all through
the 1690's, while English, Dutch, and French
diplomatists manœuvred for position and then
bargained over some compromise by partition.
The bargains failed, the Hapsburg died, and
the great War of the Spanish Succession began
in 1702, to end after a decade of bloodshed in a
partition that could have been achieved at the
outset.

That is the background before which William
Dampier played his part as an actor in the Pacific
sideshow. Dampier was a rolling stone whose
taste it was to see all countries and observe the
works of Nature. In twelve years of wandering
he drifted round the world in a variety of employ-
ments. The Pacific part of his journey was made
as a member of a crew of buccaneers, who had

37

migrated from their original West Indian habita
by reason of the increasing enforcement of law
and order in those waters. The buccaneers were
in their declining days, and the party which
Dampier joined was ill led and unenterprising
The sole interest of the expedition is that i
conveyed Dampier across the Pacific from
America to Asia, with a southward divergence
to the New Holland coast of Australia by the
way. In the East Indies he left the buccaneers
and came home to England in a merchantman.

The result was the publication in 1697 of his
*New Voyage round the World*, based upon the
journals he had kept in his twelve years' odyssey
It appeared when the Spanish succession question
was entering its crucial stage, and when by
consequence the English public were greedy for
any information about the South Sea which
would form so important a lot in the coming
auction of Spanish properties. Not only were
the English interested. The Scots were also
becoming ocean-minded, and William Paterson
was at that juncture completing the plans for
his great Scottish company to seize the isthmus
of Darien and monopolize the best link between
the South Sea and the Atlantic. The whole of
Dampier's book was interesting, but its Pacific
part was highly important; for there was a dearth
of information on the subject. The last English
book touching upon it had been the *Observations*
of Sir Richard Hawkins on his voyage of 1594

nd he had dealt only with the South American
vest coast from the Straits of Magellan to
Panama. Dampier's function was to provide
new light after a century's neglect, and his book
became a best-seller.

He himself achieved eminence, as a lion of
literary society, a useful man in the estimation
of statesmen, and an expert witness on many
matters with which the Board of Trade and
Plantations was concerned. He evinced no
desire to make financial gain from the position.
All he wanted was to go back to see some more
of the unknown and to record more observations
of the ways of savages and animals and winds
and weather, which were the main interest of
his life. He was a born scientific observer, with
more interest in an Australian aborigine than
in any fellow-Englishman. He had plenty of
courage and endurance, but no capacity for
command. The Admiralty disregarded the last
point, and made him captain of a King's ship,
to be sent on a voyage of discovery to that part
of the South Sea which Dampier thought the
most likely to yield fruitful results.

As a man of scientific mind who preferred
evidence to speculation, Dampier did not make
*Terra Australis Incognita* the main object of his
quest, but rather the unknown eastern side of
the true Australia. Tasman, by making a circular
voyage out from and home to Batavia, and by
including Australia in the circle, had proved that

it must be a great island and must have an eastern coast. But neither he nor anyone else had seen that coast. Dampier proposed to be its discoverer. He wished to sail by Cape Horn, cross the Pacific westwards as Schouten and Le Maire had done, and then push resolutely, as they had not done, to the eastern face of Australia. Official delays prevented his sailing in 1698 until it was too late to approach Cape Horn in the southern summer. Dampier could not contemplate a winter navigation of that dangerous region. With the Admiralty's consent he altered his plan and sailed by the Cape of Good Hope and the Indian Ocean, intending to reach the unknown coast by rounding northern Australia.

This was the first exploring expedition organized and equipped by the Admiralty. The organization and equipment were bad. One ship was provided instead of the two which Dampier desired and experience indicated as necessary. The ship (the *Roebuck*) was in the last stage of decay, and her rottenness was a crippling handicap to the enterprise. The crew were pressed men, lacking spirit for the adventure, and most of them neither physically fit nor experienced seamen. The officers were more inclined to play their captain false than to support him, and the first lieutenant professed open enmity and did his best to instigate a mutiny. Finally Dampier himself, although he could navigate and take scientific observations,

ould not command men. His voyages had been
hose of a subordinate, and he had never been
even a junior officer. It is surprising in these
circumstances that the *Roebuck* and her captain
got as far as they did.

Dampier sailed in January 1699. He called
at the Canaries, Cape Verdes, and Brazil, where
he left the recalcitrant lieutenant in a Portuguese
jail, and then rounded the Cape and made for
Western Australia. Here he discovered nothing
broadly new, although he amended in detail the
Dutch charting of a small extent of the coastline.
He then sailed by way of Timor round the western
end of New Guinea and along its northern coast,
for the most part out of sight of land. This
course brought him to the eastern end of the
great island and to the many lesser islands which
adjoin it. To the southward, according to the
accepted theory that New Guinea and Australia
were one land, he had the unexplored eastern
coast stretching for hundreds of miles, perhaps
as far as Tasman's Van Diemen's Land. This
was the great discovery he had come to make.
But here he turned back. He went a little way
along the southern shore of what he took to be
New Guinea and then followed a channel which
took him back to the north coast. The supposed
eastern end of New Guinea thus appeared to be
a separate island.[1] He named it New Britain

[1] It was long afterwards found to be two islands, now called
New Britain and New Ireland.

and the intervening channel Dampier's Passage and these new names on the map represent th only discoveries made by the expedition.

Dampier had valid reasons for turning back He was not a great commander, but officia stupidity had loaded him with handicaps tha probably the greatest commander could not hav overcome. One was the condition of the ship On the voyage home she vindicated Dampier b sinking in the South Atlantic, not from stress o weather but from perfection of rottenness. Al hands got safely ashore on the island of Ascension and were brought to England by ships which touched there a few weeks later. If they ha gone on down the coast of Queensland, the coas of the Barrier Reef, in such a vessel, it is safe t say that they would never have come home.

Public interest in the South Sea was now thoroughly aroused. Dampier's second book *Voyages and Discoveries*, had been published i 1699. In 1703 and 1709 he brought out th two volumes of his *Voyage to New Holland* Although he could make no good report o north-western Australia, which he confessed t be barren and repulsive, his description of New Britain was more hopeful. It was populous and productive and well placed as a base for trade northwards through the islands and for discovery southwards in the continental mysteries. People began to speak of it as a factor in novel con ceptions of a strategy of the South Sea. The

trategic point of view was emphasized by the
vents of the Spanish Succession War. The people
f Spain favoured the French candidate, the
randson of Louis XIV, and were therefore the
nemies of England in the struggle. The British
quipped privateering expeditions to raid Spanish
vealth in the Pacific, a revival of the days of
Drake. Dampier led one of these expeditions
and failed utterly. Captain Woodes Rogers led
another and succeeded brilliantly, almost in the
measure of Drake. The British government
chartered the South Sea Company in 1711. So
far as the South Sea was concerned, it never did
anything, but the public thought so highly of
its prospects that they staked and lost their
money on them in the wild gambling of the
Bubble year 1720. Further eighteenth-century
wars gave opportunity for more privateering.
In 1740 the Admiralty despatched Commodore
Anson with a squadron for a bigger purpose,
the detachment of Chile and Peru from the
Spanish empire. Anson, like Dampier, was
badly treated in the matter of equipment and
crews, and his losses on the Cape Horn passage
precluded all hopes of political effect. But he
did make a brilliant raid before crossing the
Pacific to China and capturing a Manila galleon
by the way. All these expeditions crossed the
ocean in the well-known tropical track, and
therefore made no new discoveries.

No new discovery was undertaken by the

British or the French for sixty years after Dampier had found New Britain, and this in spite of the strong popular interest in both countries. They were in fact deciding a more urgent question, that of supremacy in India, the West Indies, and North America, and in the ocean trade and sea power dependent on colonial empire. Until that struggle should be decided, as it was temporarily by the issue of the Seven Years' War in 1763, neither nation had energy to spare for the revelation of the Pacific.

Meanwhile the Russians were doing great work in the north under the leadership of the Danish captain Vitus Bering. Peter the Great sent him to far-eastern Siberia in 1725 to organize the exploration which should clear up the relationship of Asia and America. In 1728 Bering, besides charting Kamchatka and the adjoining coasts, sailed round the eastern tip of Asia and established beyond doubt that there was a strait between it and America, the Straits of Anian of the sixteenth-century theorists, now Bering Strait. For the next dozen years Bering superintended a number of expeditions for the detailed discovery of the northern coasts of Siberia. Then, in 1740–1, he crossed for the first time to the American side of his strait. He explored some part of the south coast of Alaska and died on the return passage. The incursion of Russian trappers and seal hunters into Alaska followed, but there was a gap between the

Russians and the Spaniards of southern California
which was to be left for Captain Cook's investigation.

The Dutch made a last effort at Pacific
exploration in 1721. Jacob Roggeveen sailed
by way of Cape Horn for the discovery of that
part of the southern continent which had been
reported by a buccaneer captain named Davis
as lying a few hundred miles west of Chile. This
Davis Land was imaginary, but was a factor in
the plans of more than one explorer. Roggeveen
looked for it and found only Easter Island with
its queer stone statues, which seem to have no
cultural connection with any known race of
Pacific natives. He discovered a few more islets
farther west, and then went on to Batavia, where
the Dutch East India Company seized his ships
for trespass on their monopoly.

From Dampier's time onwards the literary
interest in the South Sea continued unabated.
Dampier's writings were frequently reprinted,
separately and in collections, until he became
one of the authors whom the eighteenth century
expected to find "in every gentleman's library."
Woodes Rogers published an interesting account
of his successful privateering voyage. Other
privateers did the like. The romance of distant
travel and strange peoples seized the imagination
of the stay-at-homes, as it had done in the period
of the Renaissance. Throughout the eighteenth
century publishers found a market for multi-

volume collections of voyages, among which th
South Sea claimed a large proportion. Jonatha
Swift, seeking locations for his satirical utopia
chose regions in and round the Pacific. H
Lilliputians, treacherous, mean-minded littl
fellows—obvious Whigs—lived in unknown south
eastern Australia. Brobdingnag, the kingdom o
the giants, good-natured, sensible folk among
whom the wandering Gulliver lived very happily
was in the north-east Pacific, adjacent to th
unknown parts of California. Balnibarbi, hom
of cracked scientists and projectors, was also i
the north Pacific, but nearer to Japan. Th
Houyhnhnms, the land of equine virtue an
human depravity, occupied that part of *Terr
Australis Incognita* which fronted the Indian Ocear
All this kept the public of early Georgian Englan
in a frame of mind receptive of South Se
propaganda. The interest and its satisfactio
had also their counterparts in France.

The early eighteenth-century's idea of empir
was still rather commercial than truly colonial
Discovery was promoted and conquest under
taken not to obtain areas for settlement but t
dominate trade routes and secure the control o
rich producing-areas. "Our colonies," in th
thoughts of propagandists, existed to further th
expansion of "our commerce." It was not unti
the second half of the century that the colony
as a habitation of one's fellow-countrymen bega
to claim attention with its difficult problems o

mutual relationship, and to be recognized as such (too late to avert deplorable damage), by advanced minds like those of Burke and the elder Pitt. The interest of the post-Dampier period in the Pacific was therefore chiefly in the development of its highways and in the seizure of any valuable trading monopolies that its shores might offer.

The foundation of the South Sea Company in 1711 was an indication that the British government had in mind the commercial aspect of the Pacific. The intention was that the Company should exploit the concessions to be obtained from Spain in the forthcoming peace negotiations. In this respect the Peace of Utrecht was a disappointment, for it yielded no concessions in the Pacific and only a limited trade with Spanish colonies in the Atlantic. As a trading body the South Sea Company was always a feeble concern. After a generation it ceased to work at all in that capacity, although it prolonged its life by acting as one of the financial houses of the City of London, dealing in stocks and loans and exchanges and other such business having little direct relation with empire-building.

The attempt to gain a footing in the Pacific which had failed at Utrecht was revived in the next considerable war with Spain, that of 1739–48. It was evident that many people had been thinking and informing themselves on the subject, for as soon as war began the British government was

47

bombarded with projects and memorials. The general consensus was in favour, not of a conquest of the Pacific coasts of Spanish America (a conquest which distance would render difficult to maintain), but of assisting the Spanish colonists to liberate themselves and set up as independent states. These states would then enter into treaty relations giving trading privileges to their British benefactors. The assumption was that the colonists were sufficiently discontented to desire independence from Spain. The evidence for that may well have been exaggerated, although it proved true enough when the colonies spontaneously revolted eighty years later. But in 1740 it was not put to the test. Anson's expedition was more than half destroyed by sickness and shipwreck, and reached the west coast too weak to exercise political influence. Reluctantly he had to give up the "views" on Chile and Peru which were embodied in his secret instructions.

Anson had refreshed his depleted force at the island of Juan Fernandez, lying some 450 miles off the Chilean coast near the latitude of Valparaiso. The island had already been used by the privateers of the earlier war, one of whom was the celebrated Alexander Selkirk; and its value in the strategy of oceanic routes was recognized. Its occupation was advocated in a comprehensive South Sea scheme put forward after Anson's return. John Campbell re-edited and published in 1744 a collection of voyages which had originally been printed in the reign of Anne. In his editorial pages he outlined a national plan for the South Sea. A British force, he said—five hundred men would be sufficient—might colonize and garrison Juan Fernandez, which could thus be made impregnable to any attack by Spain. The island would serve as a port of refit and refreshment for English ships coming round Cape Horn. Being refreshed, they would proceed to sail with the south-east trades to the next seat of British power, to be established in Dampier's New Britain. A settlement here would be in the midst of populous and productive regions, New Britain itself and New Guinea, the Asiatic archipelago farther west, and the unknown eastern Australia which Dampier had been on the verge of discovering. Besides that, Campbell was quite sure that to the southward of the Juan Fernandez–New Britain track *Terra Australis Incognita* would be found and would be worth exploiting. The advantages would be great: "A new trade would be opened, which must carry off a great quantity of our goods and manufactures. . . . It would render this navigation, which is at present so strange and consequently so terrible to us, easy and familiar. . . . It would greatly increase our shipping and our seamen, which are the true and natural strength of this country."

But the British government held back. It was trying to get the war finished, for France had

joined Spain and much more than Pacific pos
sibilities was at stake. The peace, when made
proved to be a hollow affair which did not settl
the Atlantic and Indian questions at issue
Eight years of disguised war, followed by seven
more years of open war, were necessary befor
France gave over her challenge in North Americ
and India, and both countries were at last fre
to take up the South Sea enterprise in a les
bellicose and more scientific spirit than would
have moved them earlier in the century.

Meanwhile a French projector struck a new
note very different from Campbell's commercia
materialism. In 1756, just as the Seven Years
War was beginning, Charles de Brosses published
his *Histoire des Navigations aux Terres Australes*. I
gave the history of the known voyages not onl
to Australia and the South Pacific but all round
the southern hemisphere, the *Terres Australes* o
the title being *Terra Australis Incognita* in its fulles
form. De Brosses was a believer, moved both
by the historical evidence of discoveries of strang
lands and by pseudo-scientific arguments on the
balance of the earth and the means of its main
tenance. He thought that parts of the continen
would be found in temperate latitudes and tha
other parts, less favoured, would be habitabl
and useful, with a winter climate no worse tha
that of Canada. There would be a diversity o
inhabitants, some savage, some perhaps civil
ized, with a culture strange and wonderful t

50

uropeans, having grown up entirely out of
ouch with any known to them.

De Brosses went on to the advantages of
iscovering these regions. He allowed that the
ation following the enterprise would gain new
ade, but trade was by no means the greatest
ncentive. That would be the expansion of
vilization, not only by taking European know-
dge to the South but by learning much that the
outh would undoubtedly have to teach Europe.
a the mid-eighteenth century it was indeed a
old stroke of imagination to conceive that white
nen could have anything to learn from "natives,"
nd it marks De Brosses as at any rate a scholar
ith the true scholar's humility. In such vast
rritories there would be room for planting
olonies without doing wrong to the original
nhabitants; and in the pure untainted air of the
outh the social order of Europe would generate
ew vigour and virtue. These colonies would
ot be small. De Brosses pictured them in terms
nggesting the southern dominions of to-day;
nd they would have been dominions not of a
ritish but of a French Commonwealth of
ations. So morally strong would be these
oundations of a better France that Old France
ould be able to send to them her vicious and
riminal elements for purification by mere contact
ith worthiness. Such was the programme of
le Brosses, a liberal, a scholar, and a humani-
rian, and also, it is evident, a doctrinaire.

51

The beneficent enterprise of the South was
postponed by the Seven Years' War. And when
it was over, and Great Britain was for the time
the mistress of the seas, one John Callender
appropriated poor De Brosses' work and published it in English, with all the encouragements
to French enterprise altered to apply to British
and with a less than adequate acknowledgement
to the original author. But now both French
and British governments thought that the time
had come for action, and, with one notable
exception to be treated in a later chapter, the
long period of impotent projectors was at an end

Juan Fernandez had gone somewhat out of
fashion in strategical thought and had given
place to the Falkland Islands, where expeditions
on the threshold of the Pacific could be fortified
with "refreshment" before going through the
mill of the Cape Horn passage. France and
Great Britain secretly and almost simultaneously
determined to occupy the Falklands as a preliminary to South Sea enterprise. The French
acted first. In 1764 Louis Antoine de Bougainville
reached the islands with a small party of colonists
whom he planted on the shore of Berkeley Sound
In the same year the British Admiralty sent
Commodore John Byron to make a report on
the South Atlantic islands, and he arrived at the
Falklands early in 1765. Before going on to a
exploration of the Pacific he sent home his report
in consequence of which a small British colony

was established at Port Egmont in 1767. All these proceedings had been very secret. The French told no one of their colony, and Byron glanced at the islands without seeing it. The British settlers turned up without knowing that the French were there, and nearly another year elapsed before either party discovered the presence of the other. Meanwhile Spain had heard of the French settlement and protested that the islands, being part of South America, were hers. France and Spain were allies, and the French gave way, having found that the Falkland Islands were a less promising colonial site than had been supposed. Only when French officers were handing over to Spanish did the existence of the British settlement come to light. Spain requested its withdrawal, and the British government refused. In 1770 a Spanish force from Buenos Aires captured the British colonists and deported them. The Falkland Islands crisis ensued. The British government demanded restitution under threat of war. Spain was ready to fight with French assistance, but not without it; and France declined. Spain therefore gave way and restored the Falklands to Great Britain. But the British, having established the principle, did not re-establish the colony, and no one occupied the Falklands until the following century, when they did at length become a British colony. The principle established was that effective occupation outweighed mere prescriptive right, whether by prior discovery or geographical contiguity, in establishing a claim to new territories. It was a principle that had a considerable effect on the later history of the Pacific.

In the Pacific itself the decade after the Seven Years' War witnessed a series of voyages of exploration equipped by government action, most of them British but one notable exception French. All these voyages encircled the world, but the circumnavigation was incidental, and the true enterprise of each was the revelation of the Pacific.

The Falklands visit of Commodore Byron in 1765 had been only a preliminary to his main destination, which was in the Pacific. The British government was anxious to clear up the question of the North West Passage. Ships had long been passing from the Atlantic through Hudson Strait into Hudson Bay, but it was still uncertain whether a channel might exist from the Pacific to Hudson Bay or to the Arctic shore not far west of it. The results of Bering's last voyage were not perfectly known and would have been inconclusive if they had been; for he had touched at unconnected points on the south coast of Alaska, which might have been nothing but a string of islands, and he had not gone on to the coast of California. Byron was instructed to sail to the North Pacific and seek a channel through the coast of California which no English ship had visited since Drake had annexed it in the name of Queen Elizabeth. If he found a practicable passage, he was to return through it to Hudson Bay and England.

Byron entered the Pacific by the Straits of Magellan in preference to the Cape Horn route which was now becoming more usual. His reason was that scurvy grass and other edible plants could be collected in the Straits and he claimed that by their use he kept every man of his crews in health. But he took seven weeks to get through, and incurred greater risks to his ships than if he had gone round the Horn. The prevalent winds in this latitude were from the west, and the narrowness of the Straits made it almost impossible to work a large ship to windward. She was forced to wait for one of the infrequent easterly winds. The Straits also were full of dangers and ill charted, and there were few anchorages in which the hempen cables were not chafed through by rocks and the anchors lost. In modern times large steamers have used the Straits, but the sailing ships which regularly voyaged between the Atlantic and the Pacific until the opening of the Panama Canal invariably went round Cape Horn.

After passing the Straits, Byron sailed north-wards well away from the South American coast, and then turned westward to look for Davis Land (the alleged continental discovery of a seventeenth-century buccaneer) in latitude $27\frac{1}{2}°$ S. But here the winds were variable and often contrary, and

Byron did not persist. His men were now beginning to suffer from scurvy, and he determined to go nearer the equator in order to pick up the trade wind and then to cross the ocean before it, obtaining refreshment at any islands met with by the way. Byron thus completely disregarded his orders to look for the North West Passage. He crossed the equator in a long slant west-north-westwards and reached the Ladrones. Thence he went to Batavia and home by way of the Indian Ocean and the Cape. He had discovered a few small islands of no importance.

The British government now determined to search for the southern continent and gave up the problem of improving the Atlantic–Pacific highway for some years to come. In 1766 it sent out Captain Samuel Wallis in the *Dolphin*, the ship in which Byron had that year come home. With Wallis went Captain Philip Carteret in the *Swallow*—small, slow, and rotten, yet destined to make a notable voyage. Wallis was ordered to search the area west and north-west of Cape Horn, crossing the Pacific in a gradually diminishing latitude until he was within the tropics. It was the old slantwise north-westward course of so many Pacific navigators, but this time to be pursued in much more southerly latitudes. Wallis, who went through the Straits and lost Carteret in the process, did get farther west in the south Chilean latitudes than anyone else had done. But the winds then forced him northwards, so that he was very near the tropic of Capricorn before he had got 1500 miles from the South American coast. He had thus examined only a tiny fraction of the area in which the continent might lie; for the rest of his crossing was tropical, and it was fairly well known by this time that the continent was not. The tropic zone drew these expeditions like a magnet. For there was the trade-wind, fair from the eastward, and fine weather, and islands yielding fresh water and vegetables for scurvy-stricken men. The south temperate zone, by contrast, markedly colder and more tempestuous than the north temperate, gave forth variable winds, mostly foul from the west, and great seas to strain hulls and gear already weakened by a long voyage. The construction of ships and the art and science of voyaging were becoming just adequate in the later decades of the eighteenth century to complete the conquest of the Pacific; but only under the leadership of a great sailor like Cook, and not under that of the Byrons and Wallises.

In the tropical part of his passage Wallis had a stroke of luck. In 17° S. latitude, half-way between South America and New Guinea, he discovered Tahiti, the largest and most populous South Sea island reported since Tasman had sighted New Zealand. The people were not only numerous, but prosperous, intelligent, and amiable. Wallis stayed some weeks while his sick recovered and the whole crew enjoyed the attractions, fleshly and climatic, of an island paradise. At the end he was glad to sail, for everyone was getting a little out of hand. It had been a pleasant experience for explorers, whose experiences were mostly unpleasant, but Wallis could see little practical value in Tahiti. He called it King George the Third's Island. The remainder of his track round the world resembled Byron's—the Ladrones, Batavia, the Indian Ocean, and so home.

Carteret in the *Swallow* had been separated from Wallis by stress of weather at the exit from the Straits of Magellan. His ship was by far the most decayed and the worst equipped of any engaged in these eighteenth-century voyages, her condition resembling that of Dampier's *Roebuck*. She was also extremely slow, which increased the risks of scurvy and exhaustion of water on the Pacific crossing. A less spirited man than Carteret would have turned home-wards on losing the company of the senior ship, but Carteret determined to pursue the voyage alone and make his own contribution to the exploration designed by the Admiralty.

He did not keep so far west as Wallis had done after leaving the Straits, and consequently sailed over less of Davis Land in that quarter. But after watering at Masafuera, a neighbour of Juan Fernandez, he crossed more than half the Pacific in a more southerly latitude than Wallis or anyone else had kept, and so carved a slice off the theoretical continent through some sixty degrees of longitude. For Carteret discovered only small islands such as Pitcairn, but no continental land nor signs of its proximity. Keeping this southerly course, much of it in 28° S. latitude and thus outside the tropics and the trade-wind belt, was evidence of pluck and determination. It took Carteret well to the southward of Tahiti, whose refreshments would have been a reward for his hard-worked men. But at length the ship became so crazy, the supplies exhausted, and the crew so weak with scurvy, that Carteret had to seek easier conditions. He turned northwards to pick up the trade wind and then sailed approximately along the parallel which had brought Mendaña to the Solomons two centuries before.

The Spaniards had consistently understated the distance of the Solomon Islands from America, and Carteret therefore expected to find them in a position where in fact no islands existed. Not finding them, he realized that they had been so incorrectly located as to be practically lost, and sailed on, with even a suspicion in his mind that the story of their discovery was fictitious. Then in due course he came first to Santa Cruz and next to the Solomons and did not recognize what they were. This was in August 1767. Just two hundred years earlier Mendaña had led the first white men there, and in the interim none had repeated the visit. It is an illustration of the vastness of the Pacific. If anyone had found such islands in the Atlantic, how different would their story have been.

Carteret passed through the Solomons and went on to Dampier's New Britain, which also, in spite of the importance attached to it by projectors, had never been revisited since Dampier's discovery. He found that Dampier had mistaken the nature of what he had called St. George's Bay on the south coast. Instead of being a bay it was the mouth of a strait that cut north-westwards through New Britain. Carteret gave the strait the very suitable name of St. George's Channel, and called the separate island to the east of it New Ireland. He then made for Batavia to obtain an urgently needed refit. The dockyard people at that place declared that the *Swallow* should be condemned and would never reach England. But Carteret brought her home. He had made a more enterprising Pacific voyage than had Wallis, and a greater variety of discoveries. His decrepit ship had taken nearly a year longer than Wallis's *Dolphin* to complete the circumnavigation. In tracing Carteret's fortunes one feels that he was ill served. He alone of the precursors of Cook shaped as though he had it in him to do part of what Cook did, and his equipment rendered it impossible.

Bougainville, the last of these precursors, was not, like the English commanders, a professional seaman of lifelong training. He had been a university and law student, a diplomatist, and a soldier in the Seven Years' War, where he had fought in Canada under Montcalm. After the peace he had been the promoter and leader of the enterprise to colonize the Falklands as a preliminary to Pacific expansion. This had introduced him to the conduct of sea expeditions; but the conduct was obviously a general control, and for detailed knowledge and decisions he must have been dependent on his professional subordinates. There is perhaps a flavour of the amateur in his vivid descriptions of hardships and dangers which the seamen of the eighteenth century took as part of their routine and recorded without emotion.

In 1767 the share of the French in the Falklands affair came to an end with their cession of their interest to the Spaniards. Bougainville was sent out to hand over the colony and afterwards to make explorations in the Pacific. He sailed in a new frigate named the *Boudeuse* and had also with him a storeship, the *Etoile*. The two kept in company throughout the Pacific crossing, and this lightened the risks which would in many circumstances have been more serious for a solitary vessel. His instructions seem not to be on record, but the main purposes to be discerned in his proceedings were to search for the Southern Continent, particularly in the region west of Chile and Juan Fernandez (Davis Land again);

and to close with the undiscovered eastern coast of Australia.

Bougainville passed through the Straits of Magellan in January 1768, and sailed over Davis Land as Wallis and Carteret had done, his track lying about midway between theirs. Neither of the British commanders had come home when Bougainville had his last news from France, and he had to make his voyage in ignorance of what they had done. It is no detraction from his merits as an explorer that he covered, with one notable exception, much the same ground as they had done, and indeed more than once picked up information that British expeditions were ahead of him. Like Wallis, he turned westward within the tropical belt. Nearly a year after Wallis he came to Tahiti, which he named New Cythera and described in extravagant eulogy, thereby giving strong support to the cult of "the noble savage" and the return to Nature then prevalent in Paris. Although he did not use the same anchorage as the British, Bougainville heard from the natives about their visit, and knew that he was not the first discoverer. He nevertheless formally annexed the island. The British, second to occupy the Falklands, had done the like, but they had done it in ignorance that the French were there.

After leaving Tahiti, Bougainville diminished his latitude and sighted the Samoa group. He then made a radical departure from the practice of all the other commanders, except Torres, who had crossed the ocean westwards. One and all, they had kept north of New Guinea so as to make for Manila or Batavia by a known track. Torres alone had coasted south of New Guinea, and no other explorer as yet knew that he had done it; while the Australian explorations of the Dutch had given the impression that no such passage existed. To push westwards towards unknown Australia (and no one knew within a thousand miles how near or far it might be) was to take a big risk of being caught on a lee shore from which the prevailing wind might preclude escape. Bougainville took this risk, and persisted to a perilous extent before drawing back. He is entitled to higher credit than Byron or Wallis; and it must be added that he was fully conscious of the fact. His excited descriptions of danger and escape in this reconnaissance towards Torres Strait are in marked contrast to Torres's laconic account of going through the strait, with no consort to rescue him if he wrecked his ship, one hundred and sixty years before.

The more southerly course brought Bougainville first to the large island of Espiritu Santo, discovered by Quiros in 1606 and never revisited since. The northern units of the New Hebrides were adjacent, and Quiros had insisted that continental land was near. Some geographers had been drawing maps showing Espiritu Santo

as the north-eastern coast of Australia. Bougainville could see that it was part of an archipelago,
but he did not know how far it would be to the
Australian coast. He determined to probe and
see. He sailed west along the latitude of 15° S.
until he came to the outlying reefs about 150
miles from land. Shoals, rocks, and breaking seas
stretched interminably across his course. It was
an evil place in which to be caught by bad
weather. He determined to withdraw, and
turned north by east, sailing as close as possible
to the wind in order to pass round the eastern
end of New Guinea. As had happened to Torres,
this did not take him clear of New Guinea, and
he found himself in a gulf formed by the coast
of New Guinea on the one side and the great
reef fringing Australia on the other. Torres had
borne away before the wind and found his
passage through the extremity of the gulf.
Bougainville beat his way out against the wind
and finally got clear round eastern New Guinea
and its cluster of adjacent islands.

He sailed northwards through the Solomons
and failed, like Carteret, to identify them, for
they were over a thousand miles away from the
area where Mendaña's accounts seemed to place
them. Still unwittingly following Carteret, he
came next to New Britain and landed at the very
spot where the Englishman had camped and had
set up a leaden plate inscribed with details of
his visit. Natives had torn down the plate, but

Bougainville found a fragment of it, with some broken words which were evidently English but insufficient to identify the ship or her commander. Later on, at Batavia, all was explained, and Bougainville knew that it was Carteret and the little *Swallow* that he had been following. Later still, after rounding the Cape, Bougainville overtook Carteret in the Atlantic. After some civil compliments the Frenchman passed on, sailing much faster than the other. The officer whom he sent on board Carteret's ship had not revealed that the *Boudeuse* had been exploring in the Pacific, but represented her as returning from an East Indian voyage. Carteret, however, knew the truth, for one of the French boat's crew let it out in conversation with the English.

*Chapter Three*

# James Cook to the Age of Forty

COOK was forty years old when he came to his great work of exploring the Pacific. He came to it fully equipped, with his art and science already formed. In his career as an explorer we see no crude beginnings followed by improvements. He began as he went on. In technique his voyages are all of one pattern—Cook's method of conducting ocean navigations in unknown regions, a method different from those of his predecessors. His ten years' career as an explorer was the fruit of innate qualities of intellect, of an early environment about which little is known but which was evidently not detrimental to character, and of twenty years at sea divided mainly between two distinct and narrow fields of experience, the North Sea trade and the North American station of the Royal Navy. All was set in the mid-eighteenth century scene, the contest between Great Britain and the Bourbon powers for sea supremacy and oceanic empire, which was the background of the life of every sailor of Cook's age.

James Cook the navigator was born at Marton in Yorkshire on October 27, 1728. His father, also James Cook, was probably a Scot who had migrated from Roxburghshire.) There was evidently a James Cook, of about the right age, who left Roxburghshire at about the right time, although it is not yet fully proved that he was the James Cook, day labourer in Yorkshire, in whose son we are interested. The name was a common one. Later on we find three men named James Cook, entirely unrelated, all holding the rank of master in the Royal Navy, and thereby causing confusion to biographers. (The mother of the great James Cook was English. Her name was Grace Pace, and she was married to James Cook, senior, on October 10, 1725, at Stainton, near Middlesbrough.[1] )

Young Cook had been taught to read by Mrs. Mary Walker of Marton when, at the age of eight, he was sent to school by his father's employer, who thought him promising. The school is said to have taught him writing and arithmetic, but nothing further. His father was at this time made the manager or bailiff of a farm for an owner who lived elsewhere, and on this farm James Cook the younger seems to have worked from leaving school until the age of seventeen. Most likely he left school early, for it could not have taken very long to teach a boy of his intelligence writing and the elementary

[1] The relevant extract from the Stainton register has been kindly furnished to the author by Mr. Maurice Holmes.

rules of arithmetic. On those foundations Cook educated himself, continuously for the rest of his life. Probably he could have had no better education for the work he was to do. Self-tuition is inevitably narrow, but it does give self-reliance.

In 1745, at the age of seventeen or a little less, Cook went to Staithes on the Yorkshire coast to work in a grocer's shop. Research has proved fictitious the story of his having thence run away to sea with a shilling out of the till; for it is established that his employer, Mr. Saunderson, himself introduced the young man to a ship-owning firm at Whitby. There, in July 1746, James Cook was apprenticed for three years to John Walker, the head of a family firm whose principal business was to ship coal from the Northumbrian ports to London, but who also engaged in traffic with the foreign countries across the North Sea. Cook was thus about eighteen when he first went to sea, an advanced age for a sea-apprentice. It was a deliberate choice which he went out of his way to fulfil, not the pitchforking of environment which sent most sailors on board ship when they were waterside youngsters of twelve or fourteen. Cook was thus exceptional at the beginning of his sea career, as he was to remain throughout it. His appearance also must have seemed odd for a working seaman, for he was over six feet high and, to judge from his portrait, had a military stiffness of spine. His six feet were not an aid

o comfort in the living quarters of the ships of
he period, where headroom was commonly less
han that figure.

The coal trade, unlikely as it may appear at
irst sight, had valuable things to teach a future
explorer of unknown coasts. The ports of north-
east England were shallow and tidal, and the
vessels in them grounded at low water. The coal-
carrying ships were nevertheless of considerable
size, from 350 to 500 tons, and they had to be of
exceptionally strong construction to endure the
strain of taking the ground when full of cargo.
They had also to be of moderate draught in
order to make the best use of the shallow harbours
and the shallow waters of the coast. The special
qualities of ability to work in shoal water and
strength to endure grounding without damage
were thus the characteristics of these ships; and
in spite of the fact that they were not so fast or
weatherly as the minor vessels of the Navy, Cook
in after years considered them much the best
type for the exploration of uncharted coasts.
The east coast itself gave him a training different
from that of a seaman of deep-water oceanic
voyages. Every passage between London and
the coal ports was a piece of pilotage amid the
sands that fringe the coast and stretch far out
into the North Sea. The coasting sailor had to
know the channels, to recognize the landmarks,
and to predict the tidal depths and currents.
This mastery of a coastline became so much a

primary interest with Cook that in later days when in the Navy, he specialized and excelled in such work; and later still, as an explorer, he was not content to discover the existence of a new coast, but did his utmost to make a detailed survey and an accurate chart.

Cook served his three years' apprenticeship mainly in the coal trade but with occasional voyages to Norway and the Netherlands. It was the custom then for London to build up its coal stocks in the summer, and the colliers were laid up in their home ports for part at least of the winter, during which time the hands were employed in repairs and refitting. Cook as an apprentice boarded at his master's house, and there he made the most of the opportunity to study mathematics and navigation after the day's work was done. After the apprenticeship expired he sailed as an able seaman in the ships of other firms, and then in 1752 came back to the Walkers as mate of a new ship which they had just built. He continued in her until he came to the next turning-point of his life in 1755.

Meanwhile the background was very much alive, the international contest for sea power and colonies. Great Britain had gone to war with Spain on a dispute about colonial trade in 1739. Anson's incursion into the Pacific to detach Chile and Peru from the Spanish empire synchronized with other British attacks upon the Atlantic coasts of that empire, at Porto Bello

Cartagena, and the island colony of Cuba. All substantially failed, partly because after the long peace some officers were incompetent, but mainly because the obstruction, procrastination, and wrongheadedness of the administrative departments were worse than they have ever been in our history. The Spanish empire itself was not in a markedly efficient state, which rendered the failure of the attack the more humiliating. This affair merged by progressive stages into a war with France, formally declared in 1744 after considerable fighting had already taken place. Spain and France and, as a junior member, the Italian kingdom of Naples, were the Bourbon powers, ruled by different branches of the family of Louis XIV, who had fought for the Spanish succession at the beginning of the century. The two senior Bourbon powers were at war with England, mainly on colonial questions, on four successive occasions in the course of the eighteenth century.

In the war of the 1740's the British Navy retrieved the position after a bad start, and by 1747–8 had won victories which broke the French power at sea. Louisbourg, the French fortress at the mouth of the St. Lawrence, was taken, and the British command of the sea was so powerful that if the war had continued all the French interests in Canada, the Caribbean, and India would have been in peril. At the same time the French armies in Europe had been highly

71

successful and had virtually conquered the southern or Belgian Netherlands. French power in Antwerp, and perhaps later in Amsterdam, was an unpleasant prospect for the British. At Aix-la-Chapelle in 1748 both sides agreed to a peace of restitution, the French to save their overseas empire, the British as the only means of getting the French army out of the Netherlands. Between France and England all conquests were given up. Between Spain and England there were no conquests to give up.

The respective governments in Europe sincerely meant to make peace, but in America and India the treaty of 1748 was only the prelude to a new period of irregular war. In the first year of the so-called peace Dupleix began his attempts to dominate Indian provinces and drive the British from their factories. At the same time in North America both the French and the British made aggressive moves, either side striving to monopolize the Ohio valley and evict the other. The Indian affair was comparatively innocuous, for Dupleix was disavowed and recalled by his own government in 1753. But in America the fighting grew ever more serious, and merged from local and unofficial hostilities into regular operations directed from Europe. By 1754 the French were in possession of the Ohio valley. The British government declared it to be a violent intrusion on British territory and sent out General Braddock with some regular troops to stiffen the colonial militia. In 1755 Braddock was ambushed, defeated, and killed while marching towards the Ohio. The Indian allies of the French took the warpath along the whole British frontier, and many farms were destroyed and settlers killed. A French fleet and military reinforcements sailed for Canada. A British fleet followed and made an indecisive attempt to intercept them. Privateers of both countries captured numbers of merchantmen at sea. All this took place without declaration of war, which was not made until the summer of 1756. But the Seven Years' War in fact began in 1755.

The Navy was placed on a war footing, which meant fitting out ships that had been laid up for years and expanding the personnel four or fivefold by impressing merchant seamen and landsmen. There was a "hot press" in all the seaports at the midsummer of 1755.

Cook had just been offered the command of the Walkers' ship in which he was serving as mate. He declined it and determined to join the Navy. It had been said that he volunteered in order to avoid being impressed. But this is incorrect, for he could, if he had chosen, have been master of a merchantman, and as such would have been exempt from impressment. In fact he made a free choice, natural to an able man of twenty-seven. A naval war was beginning and would last for years. Cook, as he himself said, "had a mind to try his fortune that way."

He had to join as an able seaman, but had no fear of remaining long without promotion. Men such as he were at a premium for licking into shape the depressed and unhandy landsmen who formed the major part of the takings of the press-gang. He joined the service in London on June 17 and was sent on board the 60-gun ship *Eagle* at Portsmouth on June 25. A month later he was made master's mate. Six months later still he became boatswain, a position of some responsibility in a large ship.

For two years Cook served in the *Eagle*, cruising in home waters in maintenance of the blockade of the French coast. During the greater part of this time he was under the command of Captain Hugh Palliser, who discerned his qualities and recommended him for promotion. Cook's former employers at Whitby urged his merits upon the local Member of Parliament, who said a word for him at the Admiralty. This was the eighteenth-century method of advancing the right man. It was equally effective in advancing the wrong man, as frequently happened; but in Cook's case there could be no suggestion of favouritism or corrupt influence because he had nothing to recommend him but his own worth. There had, however, been scandals about the promotion of mere children of influential parents to commissioned rank. The Admiralty was therefore enforcing a regula-tion that no commission should be granted to anyone who had not six years' service in the King's ships; and so Cook had to wait.

The blockade involved prolonged cruising in the Channel and Irish waters, chasing and stopping suspected vessels, and one serious action with a heavily armed ship, resulting in her capture after the *Eagle* had suffered forty-two casualties. Cook was sometimes sent on detached duty in command of small craft, and on one occasion was put in command of a large prize which he brought into the Thames. Naval hygiene gave him food for thought, as his subsequent career was to show. On one summer cruise in home waters the *Eagle* buried 22 men in a month from sickness, and sent 130 more into hospital on arrival in port. It was not only the food that was to blame, but wet and unventilated quarters, lack of proper clothing, and recruitment of unfit men.

In July 1757, just over two years after joining the Navy, Cook was made master of the *Solebay* and later of the *Pembroke*, a 64-gun ship-of-the-line. The master was a warrant officer whose duties included the navigation and pilotage of the ship and the general control of the crew and their work. Such a man had necessarily to have expert knowledge of all that pertained to the duties of those under him and also some skill in the science of navigation, which was a mystery to nearly all the lower deck and by no means a familiar study with many of the officers. That

Cook should have attained this position in s
short a time shows that men thought well of him

His important naval service began in 1758
when the *Pembroke* joined the fleet which con
veyed the army of Wolfe and Amherst to Nort
America. In 1756-7 the British had had th
worst of the contest with the French in Canada
and the fighting had for the most part take
place within the borders of the British colonie
William Pitt, who gained control of the Britis
war effort in 1757, determined to conque
Canada, if possible in one campaign. For 175
he planned expeditions to evict the French fron
the Ohio country, to strike north from New Yor
to the St. Lawrence, and to capture Louisbour
and afterwards ascend the St. Lawrence and tak
Quebec. The first of these undertakings suc
ceeded, the second failed, and in the third Coo
bore his subordinate part.

Louisbourg was a fortified harbour on Cap
Breton Island at the entrance to the Gulf
St. Lawrence. It formed a secure base for
French fleet, and its capture was essential befor
a British expedition could go on to Quebe
Wolfe led the soldiers who landed from sma
boats on fortified beaches and stormed their wa
across entrenchments to the landward defence
of Louisbourg. Cook was not present at th
landing, for his ship had remained at Halifa
but he arrived in time to take part in the sieg
that followed. It endured for a month, and i

st transaction was an attack by the boats of
e British fleet upon the French ships guarding
e entrance of the harbour. The *Pembroke*
ntributed her boats, but it seems unlikely that
ook went with them, for the master's duty was
n board his own ship. The attack was success-
l, and Louisbourg surrendered immediately
fterwards. The move upon Quebec had then
o be postponed to the following year. Bad
eather had protracted the outward passage of
e expedition from England to eleven weeks,
nd the siege of Louisbourg had taken four
ore. There was not enough of the season left
o tackle Quebec with any hope of success. The
eet patrolled and reconnoitred the Gulf of
t. Lawrence and returned to Halifax to winter
nd refit.

Next year, 1759, was made famous by Wolfe's
apture of Quebec. The story used to be told
olely in terms of the Army's achievements.
Modern research has brought out the remarkable
fficiency and enterprise of the Navy, without
hich the soldiers would never have seen Quebec.
Only once before had the British seen it—in
629, when Quebec itself had been but a village
nd had surrendered to a handful of English
rivateers ascending the river in small craft.
Charles I restored it to the French three years
ater. In 1711, when Quebec was well fortified
nd garrisoned, a regular expedition sailed from
ngland to take it, an expedition of 5000 troops

conveyed by numerous transports and twent
ships-of-war. The result was one of the fev
failures of the War of the Spanish Succession, bu
it was a very complete failure. In the S
Lawrence estuary the ships were entangle
among shoals and reefs. There was no skille
pilotage, and many were wrecked. After 80
lives had been lost the expedition withdrew, no
having come anywhere near Quebec or attempte
the most difficult part of the passage, which la
nearest to the city. Half a century had passe
since then, but the memory of failure and in
competence still rankled, and the fleet of 175
was on its mettle to carry a Quebec expeditio
to success.

Pitt appointed Sir Charles Saunders to th
command. He arrived at Halifax in April, t
find that the local squadron, in which Cook wa
serving, had already lost a point to the enemy
The winter had been unusually severe and pro
longed, and the ice in the St. Lawrence was lat
in breaking up. A French squadron with re
inforcements for Quebec timed its appearanc
just as the river became open and before th
British were alive to the fact. Quebec was thu
the stronger by some useful soldiers, includin
Bougainville the future navigator, who migh
have been intercepted in the approaches. Afte
this all was energy, and Saunders and Wolf
inspired every man to do his utmost.

The result was that skilled and zealous wor

was applied to sounding the channels and charting the reefs and shoals. French charts and pilots had been captured, but no great reliance was placed on them, for the French themselves had never taken battleships up to Quebec. The boats of the British fleet did all the surveying as if it were a piece of new discovery, and the channels were buoyed and marked in advance of the great ships. The masters of the fleet were to the fore in this work, for they were the specialists in pilotage. Cook attracted notice for his efficiency in the survey, particularly in a difficult part known as the Traverse, in which the channel shifted from the north to the south side of the river amid a maze of dangerous obstructions. When all was done the expedition sailed safely up to the Isle of Orleans, just below the city, where the base of the siege operations was established. From there the survey was extended close to the Quebec shore and up river beyond the city, where Wolfe ultimately made his successful landing. The story of the taking of Quebec is not relevant to this chapter, which is concerned with Cook's personal record. He bore his part in all the boat work, which included a good deal of skirmishing with similar French boat parties, and constant vigilance against fireships. On one occasion we see him being consulted by Wolfe about the approach to a landing place, and the contemporary writers on the campaign referred to him as the master surveyor and master of the fleet, titles which were quite unofficial but significant of his reputation.

Quebec fell in September, 1759, and before the end of the month the greater part of the fleet sailed for England. A few ships were left in North American waters under Lord Colville, and Cook was transferred as master to his flagship the *Northumberland*. The St. Lawrence and its gulf were now a British conquest, and a proper survey of many unknown shores and channels was necessary. There is no doubt that Cook was retained with this purpose in view. When the river froze, Colville's ships retired to Halifax, the usually ice-free Nova Scotian port, and in the spring of 1760 they were in the St. Lawrence as soon as it was possible. It was fortunate that they had been left close at hand, for during this winter the British garrison of Quebec was hard pressed. Only a small force had been left to hold the place and the French had closed on it from all over Canada. In May the troops were sick, starving, and barely able to hold their lines. If a French fleet had come first up the river as in the previous year they would probably have been obliged to surrender, and Wolfe's victory would have been in vain. But the first ships up were British, and the besiegers withdrew, to be hemmed in in their turn that summer and compelled to surrender at Montreal in September.

Cook studied hard during the winter at Halifax fitting himself for the scientifically accurate work he was now to undertake. The sounding and ketch-chart making done hurriedly and sometimes under fire in the campaign of 1759 had called for courage and intelligence but not for more book-learning than any of Cook's fellow-masters could display. Surveying and charting by trigonometrical methods leading, as they did, to the preparation of charts which had not been superseded after the lapse of a century were work that no one else on the station could have performed. Cook had no instructor. He taught himself from books. No one but himself had ever taught him how to read such works as those which he must now have mastered. The horn-book at the village school was the limit of his studies under tuition, and it had not given much guidance to the reading of pure and applied mathematics. His intellect was great, but his character was greater. He was in a class that has no counterpart in these days, certainly not comparable with the sheltered and scholarship-ed youth who now carry on the lamp of knowledge.

The summer of 1760 saw Cook chiefly engaged in surveying the St. Lawrence, and in the next two seasons he was at the same task on parts of the Nova Scotian and Newfoundland coasts. His commanding officer, Lord Colville, reported on him in generous terms, the Admiralty became aware that they had a man of "genius and capacity . . . for greater undertakings of the

same kind," and some of his work was published
All this did not bring a commission, even with
the necessary six years' service. Quite possibly
Cook did not desire one. As master of a battle
ship he was well paid in relation to his modes
needs—at the end of this year 1762 he had nearly
three hundred pounds due to him on leaving the
*Northumberland*; and he may have been in a
better position to dispose of his time and order
his own work than a junior officer would have
been. His highly placed friends would certainly
have pushed his claim with success if they had
been urged to do so. At this very time there
was another and quite undistinguished James
Cook, also a master in the Navy, who was granted
a lieutenant's commission and continued placidly
to hold that rank for forty years to come.

In November, 1762, the *Northumberland* returned
to England, and Cook was paid off after a service
of nearly five years in North America. He was
now thirty-four, and in the following month he
married Elizabeth Batts. She belonged to a
family of craftsmen and tradesmen dwelling
about the Thames waterside. The marriage took
place at Shadwell, and the bride was described
as of Barking. There is no evidence that Cook
had known her before the war, when in any case
she was little more than a child, for she was
only twenty-one in 1762. So it looks as though
the courtship was a brief and brisk affair. They
took a house in Shadwell and thence moved to

more permanent home in Mile End; and for
time Cook was able to enjoy more domestic
e than fell to the lot of most sailors. For the
ext five years he was to be regularly away every
mmer and home in England every winter.
rs. Cook produced a family with almost corre-
onding regularity, and all proceeded with
ethod and harmony save that one of the infants
fused to play its part by surviving infancy, and
o more died in childhood. But that was
mmon form in the eighteenth century, and
ere were three survivors, all boys.

Early in 1763 the Treaty of Paris terminated
e Seven Years' War, but Cook nevertheless
turned to Newfoundland. The new governor
that colony, Captain Thomas Graves, was
gent that the task of surveying and charting
e coasts should be completed. Cook was
pointed surveyor at 10s. a day, which was
ore than the pay of a master. He was allowed
assistant and a good set of instruments, and
rried on the work in a small vessel purchased
Newfoundland. He is officially referred to as
Mr. James Cook, Engineer," and again as "the
ing's Surveyor," and his status seems to have
en exceptional. Although not a commissioned
ficer, he was a man of mark and high standing.
His first task was carried out as a race against
ne. The islands of St. Pierre and Miquelon
re to be restored to the French by the terms
the Treaty, but the Admiralty desired first

83

to have their coasts charted. Unfortunately t
French officer who was to take them over arriv
at the same time as Cook. He was according
kept waiting by all the resources of red tap
unfortunate absence of indispensable person
reference to distant authorities, lengthy a
leisurely correspondence, and suchlike devic
until he grew very angry indeed. Meanwh
Cook, working at high pressure, carried out t
survey, and the islands returned to the hands
the French with none of their secrets unknov
to the British.

Sir Hugh Palliser, Cook's old captain in t
*Eagle*, became governor of Newfoundland in 176
He proved himself a firm friend and did mu
to facilitate Cook's work, the charting
minutely accurate methods of section after secti
of the Newfoundland coast. Palliser provid
Cook with a schooner, the *Grenville*, which w
established as an independent vessel with 1
own crew, instead of being manned by detac
ments from the flagship as the surveying cr
had hitherto been. Cook was thus able to s
his ship home to England for the winter inste
of taking any passage that offered in the lar
vessels that might be returning. He continu
to do this each year, laying-up the *Grenville*
the Thames, and going to his home to work
four months on the charts that recorded
results of the previous season's surveying.
August 1766 Cook made observations of

eclipse of the sun visible in Newfoundland. The chronometer was at that time just being perfected by John Harrison and was not yet in general use, and accurate records of eclipses were the best means of fixing the longitudes of the places at which they occurred. Cook made a report which was communicated to the Royal Society and gave him an introduction to that body which was to be useful in smoothing his path at a later juncture. The Royal Society's *Transactions* referred to him as "Mr. Cook, a good mathematician, very expert in his business." Such words from that source were certainly the equivalent of an honours degree in mathematics to-day. The fact that his assistant in the survey was that year commissioned lieutenant served to emphasize his own unique position.

Cook brought the *Grenville* home for the last time in the winter of 1767–8. As usual, he worked up his results, with the apparent prospect of returning in the spring to Newfoundland. But larger circumstances were now enfolding his career, and he was destined to see Newfoundland no more.

*Chapter Four*

# Preliminaries to the First Pacific Voyage

ALEXANDER DALRYMPLE, Fellow of the Royal Society, at the age of thirty was a man of many parts. He had been at Madras in the service of the East India Company. He had then gone to sea, still in their service, and had risen to the command of a merchantman in Far Eastern waters. Like Cook, he had learnt surveying and navigation and was a competen astronomer. He had studied the history of South Sea discovery and had made an important contribution to it by his own research; for at Madras before the siege of that place by the French in 1759, he had come upon a document which proved that a strait existed between New Guinea and Australia and that Luis Vaez de Torres had sailed through it a hundred and fifty years before It was the first evidence ever brought to light of the existence of Torres Strait, the strait which the Dutch explorers had declared to be non existent. Dalrymple returned to England 1765 and set about writing a small volume South Sea discoveries, embodying his ow historical discovery about Torres. He had this book printed in 1767, but delayed its publication for another two years.

In the course of his studies Dalrymple became a believer in the unknown southern continent in the extremest form in which it was possible to hold that belief in the eighteenth century. He did not, of course, claim that Australia was part of it. But he did accept Tasman's theory that New Zealand was. He accepted also the story of Davis Land over towards the Chilean side of the South Pacific. Between the two, and farther north than either of them, he accepted Quiros's assertion of a continental coast. For the very large intervals between the sites of these main assertions there was no evidence at all, but Dalrymple unhesitatingly filled the gaps with land. By linking all together he obtained an immense continent with a northern shore extending for thousands of miles on the edge of the tropics, and with a boundless interior covering very south temperate latitude and all the antarctic into the bargain. That Dalrymple, a man of intellect and wide experience, should have accepted a conclusion for which the evidences were so feeble and scanty, is an index of his character. He was domineering and overbearing to the point of eccentricity, and he allowed himself to form prejudices which he maintained with an obstinacy impervious to reason. His master prejudice was the belief in the great continent.

He considered himself its intellectual discoverer
and he determined to be its physical discoverer
He was ready to command an expedition to the
south and to sail courses that other commander
had found too difficult.

So much has been said about him here, no
only because he was a promoter of Pacific dis
covery, but also because he became a seriou
candidate for the command of the great under
taking that was about to take shape. In th
outcome the command did not fall to him bu
to Cook, who, so far as we know, had hithert
evinced no special interest in the problems of th
South Sea. Between the ardent enthusiast an
the cool professional, there was a contras
heightened, as not often in real affairs, by th
rejection of the candidate who believed so full
in the unknown continent and the acceptanc
of him who was to prove by dispassiona
investigation that no such continent existed.

It will be remembered that in 1766 Callend
had published his English paraphrase of th
persuasive work of Charles de Brosses. In Ma
of that year Byron had come home, with litt
to report, it is true, but that he had made
voyage across the Pacific. It was, however, th
first time for almost a quarter of a century th
a British ship had done as much, and publ
interest was stimulated. The sailing of Wall
and Carteret followed, but in the winter
1767–8, with whose events we are now concerne

neither of those captains had returned. Wallis, the first to appear, arrived on May 20, 1768. Carteret reached England and Bougainville France both in March, 1769, and their experiences bore no part in shaping the intentions of Cook's first Pacific voyage.

The transit of the planet Venus across the face of the sun was a rare event first observed by Jeremiah Horrocks in Lancashire in 1639. Early in the eighteenth century Edmund Halley, the Astronomer Royal, calculated that it would occur again in 1761 and probably in 1769, and thereafter no more for a century. By accurate observations of the transit taken from widely distant points on the earth's surface astronomers hoped to obtain the distance of the earth from the sun. In 1761 some observations were taken, but others failed owing to cloudy weather, and the data obtained were insufficient for the purpose in view. But the 1761 observations did provide a basis for the prediction of the exact circumstances of the transit of 1769. The whole scientific world was interested, and the Royal Society determined to make the most of the occasion. In November 1767 the Society appointed a committee to consider the question. It included Nevil Maskelyne, the Astronomer Royal, and other acknowledged authorities. Their calculations showed that stations near the North Cape of Norway and in Hudson Bay would provide observations from a northern latitude, while the contrasting southern observations could be obtained only from an area bisected by the tropic of Capricorn and roughly half-way across the Pacific from Chile to the Dutch Indies. If the transit was to be usefully observed a scientific voyage to the South Pacific would thus be necessary. Armed with these facts, the Royal Society appealed to King George III for his royal aid and patronage; and the King, ever a friend to enlightened projects, promised £4,000 and the provision of a ship by the Navy. It is important to note the date, February 29, 1768, by which this decision had been taken. On that day Lord Shelburne, Secretary of State, formally notified the Admiralty that by the King's desire it was to provide a ship for the Pacific expedition.

It occurred to more than one party that this expedition could fulfil other purposes beside those of astronomy. Dalrymple was a competent astronomer and he was also, in his own mind, the prospective discoverer of the unknown southern continent. He was in some sense a seaman, although his sea experience had not accounted for a great deal of his time; and he had been for a short period in command. As astronomer, sailor, and geographer he considered himself qualified to command the Society's expedition, and to achieve its objects and afterwards his own ambitions. He was himself a member of the Society, and he had the backing of the Astronomer

Royal. The Society could think of no one better, and his appointment seemed to be a foregone conclusion.

But the men of science were reckoning without the Admiralty. It was to provide the indispensable ship, and it also had motives ulterior to the observation of the transit. Broadly its motives were those of Dalrymple, but it would have phrased them differently. Dalrymple, in his own conceit, was going to discover and explore the southern continent. The Admiralty's expedition was to see whether there was a southern continent. Most likely on account of his cocksureness and his hectoring and unpleasant personality, the Admiralty decided that Dalrymple should not command. There were two quotable precedents against the command of a King's ship by a civilian, those of Edmund Halley, above mentioned, and of Dampier. Halley had been made temporary captain of a ship in order to take a series of observations at sea on the question of longitude, and his scientific eminence had not prevented his subordinates from mutinying against his amateur authority. Dampier, ex-buccaneer and student of natural history, had also provoked something like a mutiny, and a court-martial had found him guilty of ill-treating his first lieutenant and had declared him unfit to command. There was, however, no need to cite precedents, for, as we have already seen in Cook's case, a regulation debarred any

man from a commission in the Navy who had
not already served for six years in some non-
commissioned capacity. These things considered
the Admiralty refused to appoint any but a naval
officer to the command. The decision was made
known by the president to the council of the
Society on March 24, but it had been reached
earlier in the month. Although a naval officer
was to command the expedition, the Society
still had the appointment of the scientific staff
and it pressed Dalrymple to go as chief observer
of the transit. He was not attracted. The
transit meant very little to him, and he had no
mind to be a mere observer of the achievement
of a King's officer in discovering and exploring
*his* continent. He refused to go in any capacity
except that of commander of the whole undertaking.

The Admiralty had already made its own choice,
that of Cook. He was not a commissioned officer
but he could immediately be made one, and in
his case the promotion was long overdue. The
interesting point, interesting because it bears on
the selection of the famous *Endeavour*, is, when
did the Admiralty decide on Cook? At the end
of February it knew that it was to provide a ship
and the question of a commander must at once
have arisen, for it was obviously the more
important of two complementary decisions—the
ship and her captain—that had to be made.
On March 4 Cook attended to report the result

"ENDEAVOUR"

of his previous season's work in Newfoundland. For the rest of the month he was busied in fitting out the *Grenville* for her next voyage to the same destination. Some have argued that this shows that Cook was unconscious of any other possibilities, but the contention is valueless. Whatever he knew, a man like Cook, disciplined and methodical, would faithfully have carried out his existing duties until formally relieved of them. But there is no written evidence, and it is not until April 6 that we hear definitely that Cook's appointment had, at some previous date, been made. On that day Palliser asked for a new master to be sent to the *Grenville* in place of Cook, who "is to be employed elsewhere." That is about all, and it is possible to believe that Cook was chosen only a few days before this remark was made ; but it is also possible that the choice was made a month earlier.

All this brings us to the ship. Cook's *Endeavour* is one of the famous ships of history, like Columbus's *Santa Maria*, Magellan's *Victoria*, Drake's *Golden Hind*, and the Pilgrim Fathers' *Mayflower*; and she is unlike her noble predecessors in being exactly known. No one knows the true appearance, the lines of the hull, the details of the rig, or even the primary dimensions, of the *Santa Maria*, the *Victoria*, the *Golden Hind*, or the *Mayflower*; and even the most impressive models of these ships are only guesswork applied to general knowledge, a fact concerning which the catalogues

C.O.P.—4*

of museums are not always candid. But the *Endeavour* is well documented. Her lines exist, sheer-draft, waterlines and body-plan as they were recorded for official reference; a specification of her masts and spars; plans of her cabin arrangements as reconstructed for the great voyage; and dimensions not only of the ship in the large but of many details of the construction. Even the painting and varnishing are on record. The model made under Admiralty direction from these particulars is a true portrait.

The *Endeavour* was a Whitby collier, the kind of ship in which Cook had passed his early years at sea. It is tempting to believe that he, from his knowledge of the type, selected it for the work he had to do. It is easily credible, and it is even highly probable, but it is not a perfectly proven fact. He himself wrote, on the qualities desirable in a ship to be used for exploration:

A ship of this kind must not be of a great draught of water, yet of a sufficient burden and capacity to carry a proper quantity of provisions and necessaries for her complement of men, and for the term requisite to perform the voyage. She must also be of a construction that will bear to take the ground, and of a size which, in case of necessity, may be safely and conveniently laid on shore to repair any accidental damage or defect. These properties are not to be found in ships of war of forty guns, nor in frigates, nor in East India Company's ships, nor in large three-decked W

India ships, nor indeed in any other but North-country ships such as are built for the coal trade, which are peculiarly adapted for this purpose.

But Cook wrote this three years later, and although it shows that the choice of the *Endeavour* would have been his own, it does not prove that he was consulted in 1768. The question turns on the dates. We do not know when Cook was selected for the command, but we do know when the ship was chosen. On March 5 the Admiralty notified the Navy Board, which dealt with dock-yard work and the provision of ships, that a vessel would be wanted for exploration. The Navy Board replied on March 8 that the *Tryal* was suitable, but could not be made ready before the end of May. On the 10th the Admiralty wrote that this would be too late and directed the Navy Board to report on the *Rose*. No answer is on record until the 21st, when the Navy Board wrote that the *Rose* was not capable of stowing the quantity of provisions requisite for the voyage. But, they went on to say, their lordships might consider a cat-built vessel (i.e., in this context, a collier), a type which "are roomly and will afford the advantage of stowing and carrying a large quantity of provisions so necessary on such voyages, and in this respect preferable to a ship of war." If so, there is such a ship at present available in the Thames. Now, the Navy Board are here saying much the same about stowage and superiority to a ship of war as Cook said in the extract quoted above. Is it not very likely that the Navy Board had been talking to Cook and had adopted his views? It seems possible also that the Admiralty had already accepted these views, for it answered on the same day, directing the purchase of the vessel in question. On the whole it looks very probable that Cook was appointed, at least informally, between March 10 and March 21, that he was consulted about the choice of a ship, and that his recommendation was for a cat-built North Country collier. But "very probable" is as far as we can go.

There were in fact several colliers then in the Thames, and the Navy Board inspected them all. By March 29 the choice was made and the vessel called the *Earl of Pembroke* purchased. She was renamed the *Endeavour*, and since the Navy already had a vessel of that name, she was officially called the *Endeavour Bark*. This has led to some misapprehension and even caused Mr. A. Kitson, whose biography is the foundation of the modern study of Cook, to go astray. For he, with others, was tempted to equate "bark" with "barque." The modern word "barque" descriptive of a particular rig, a technical term with an exact meaning. The older word "bark" is much less exact, had different shades of meaning at different periods, and applied to the vessel as a whole and not to her rig. There was a trasitional period in which the meaning might be the old or the new. But in Cook's case the connotation is obvious, for the *Endeavour* was not rigged as a barque. The Navy, already possessing a fighting *Endeavour*, had now acquired a merchantman and given her that name. "Bark" therefore designates a minor, subsidiary vessel; and that is the meaning frequently attached to it from the sixteenth century onwards. That "bark" was not, like "barque," a term of technical exactness, is illustrated by the fact that when two more Whitby colliers of the same type were taken into the Navy for Cook's second voyage, they were officially described, not as barks, but as sloops. Kitson unfortunately got a picture of a nineteenth-century barque and reproduced it as "typical of the *Endeavour*." It was very unlike the real *Endeavour* as revealed by her contemporary plans; but they had not come to light when Kitson wrote in 1907.

Cook's *Endeavour* was of 368 tons, built at Whitby in 1764. The term "cat-built" is of Scandinavian origin, and the English colliers so described were of enormously strong construction, great stowage capacity, and comparatively shallow draught. These qualities were only achieved at the expense of speed. The *Endeavour's* lines show her body to have been very full for the greater part of her length, her mid-section almost rectangular, and her ends short and snubbed. Such a ship could be neither so fast nor so weatherly as the lighter ships of the Navy, whose speed and capacity for sailing close to the wind were part of their fighting qualities. But Cook, in praising the collier type for exploration, was not thinking of rapid passages across the oceans but rather of the coasting work to be done on arrival. Neither was he contemplating the type of expedition which killed thirty per cent. of its personnel by hardships and scarcities which he considered avoidable. Hence his insistence on that "capacity to carry a proper quantity of provisions and necessaries" as being so indispensable. This line of thought was original and independent, for hitherto it had been assumed that the ideal explorer's ship was a fast frigate such as Bougainville's *Boudeuse*. The *Endeavour* was ship rigged and was fitted to mount a few light guns. The dockyard made considerable alterations in her accommodation in order to provide for the large crew and the scientific staff who would sail in her. Her sides and lower masts were finished bright with pine varnish, and her spars were coloured black.

The Admiralty having settled the command and the commander having (most probably) decided on the ship, it remained for the Royal Society to make the scientific appointment. There were to be two qualified astronomers to observe the transit. The Society, having knowledge of Cook's competence in this matter from his previous work on the eclipse of the sun

98

ppointed him as one of the observers and
Charles Green, an assistant to the Astronomer
Royal, as the other. May 5, the date of this
ppointment, was the first occasion on which
Cook attended the Society's council in person.
They were favourably impressed and agreed to
ay him a substantial fee and provide the neces-
ary instruments. Towards the end of the month
e received his commission as lieutenant, and
egan to make ready for sea. Astronomy, how-
ver, was not the only science in prospect. Joseph
Banks, twenty-four years of age, a botanist of
epute, a Fellow of the Royal Society, and a rich
nan, desired to accompany the expedition with
cientific assistants and personal servants. The
ociety earnestly requested the Admiralty to
llow this, and the request was granted, Banks
eing a friend of Lord Sandwich, the First Lord.
His assistants included Dr. Solander, a botanist,
nd Alexander Buchan, an artist.[1] Young Banks
as quite unspoiled by wealth. He proved to be
ardy, cheerful, and a good sportsman, with a
air for dealing with savages. He and Cook
ecame firm friends, and his presence was
rtainly no detriment to the discipline and con-
ntment of the expedition.

The material preparations included the struc-
ral alterations to the *Endeavour*, noted above,
e replacement of some of her spars, and the

[1] In 1946 it is necessary to explain that this does not mean
performer.

sheathing of her hull for protection against the boring worm of tropical waters. In the coasting trade ships were not sheathed, as the worm of our latitudes is comparatively harmless. But in the tropics worm could virtually destroy a ship in a brief period unless precautions were taken. They consisted in coating the underwater parts with an extra skin of planking, beneath which was a layer of tarred felt, impermeable to worm. The outer planking was liable to destruction, and its renewal was periodically necessary. At this time copper sheathing was being experimented with; but it was thin and easily torn away, and Cook preferred the old sheathing for a voyage to remote parts where repairs to the copper would be difficult. The extensive work done on the *Endeavour* cost almost as much as her purchase price. It shows that the Admiralty was doing its best for the expedition, and contrasts with the treatment of Dampier seventy years before. Victuals for eighteen months were put on board, including some things not usually taken to sea, and clothing and other stores were allowed on a liberal scale. Byron's crew had suffered badly from scurvy, and Cook had ideas for its prevention. The Admiralty gave him the means of carrying them out.

As explorers' stores Cook carried copies of all the available writings on the Pacific, the most recent being the log of Captain Wallis, who reached England on May 20, 1768. Dalrymple

sore though he was at what he considered his
unjust supersession, gave Banks a copy of his
printed but unpublished volume containing the
evidence for the existence of Torres Strait.
Dalrymple apparently could not bring himself
to communicate with Cook, whom, in his pre-
judiced way, he treated as personally responsible
for intriguing him out of the command; but he
knew that Banks would show the volume to Cook
and so can be credited with a certain generosity.
The book contained also the pseudo-evidence
for the Southern Continent which Dalrymple
now expected Cook to find; in which happy
event the author would be in a position to say,
"Just as I told him! He has merely followed my
directions"; so that the generosity was not
unmixed with self-gratification. The most important news that Wallis had brought was that
of the discovery of Tahiti, well within the area
in which the astronomical observations were to
be made. A prolonged stay at Tahiti was therefore embodied in the instructions drawn up for
Cook.

Those instructions were devised in great detail
and were issued by the Admiralty on July 30.
Like all such documents the instructions were
secret at the time; and they remained so, long
after the need for secrecy had passed, simply
because no one displayed the curiosity to look
for them. They were at length found and
published by the Navy Records Society in 1928.

101

Cook was ordered to go to Tahiti by the Cape Horn route, with permission to touch at certain places by the way. He was to reach Tahiti at least a month before June 3, 1769, the date of the transit, in order that full preparations should be made. At the proper time he was to ensure that the scientific work should be carried out. Next, he was to sail southwards from Tahiti as far as 40° S. in search of the southern continent which "there is reason to imagine" may be found. If it was not found, he was to turn westward, sailing between 40° and 35° until he should reach the unknown eastern side of the land discovered by Tasman and now called New Zealand. He was to explore the coast of New Zealand as fully as possible and thence make for some port where provisions could be obtained for the return voyage to England, to be made, at Cook's discretion, by Cape Horn or the Cape of Good Hope.

The southern continent was in the Admiralty's view the main object of the voyage, and the work to be done on it, if found, was elaborately specified. The coast was to be explored, surveyed, and charted. The nature of the soil was to be examined, and report made on all animal, vegetable, and mineral products, specimens being collected and brought home. "You are likewise to observe the genius, temper, disposition and number of the natives, if there be any, and endeavour by all proper means to cultivate a friendship and alliance with them, making them presents of such traffic, and shewing them every kind of civility and regard; taking care, however, not to suffer yourself to be surprised by them, but to be always upon your guard against any accidents. You are also with the consent of the natives to take possession of convenient situations in the country, in the name of the King of Great Britain; or, if you find the country uninhabited, take possession for His Majesty by setting up proper marks and descriptions, as first discoverers and possessors."

The plain fact was that if a populous continent existed, with its people at a reasonably advanced economic level, its future relationship with the rest of the world was a life-and-death interest to the British people. Should it fall to the French and their Spanish satellites to exploit the empire-building of a vast sub-tropical region, they would obtain such an accession of sea power that British enterprise would be squeezed out not only of the Pacific but of all the other oceans. Already British industry dependent on trans-oceanic markets was employing an appreciable part of the population. The prospect of a Bourbon maritime supremacy meant ultimate ruin. In the possible exploitation of a southern continent England could not afford to be left out. And so Cook sailed, bearing in his capable hands not only the interests of science but the fortunes of his country.

*Chapter Five*

# The First Voyage: Tahiti and New Zealand

WHEN all was at length in readiness Cook quitted the Thames for Plymouth, and from that port sailed finally on August 25, 1768. On board the *Endeavour* there were seventy-one officers and sailors, twelve marines, and eleven landsmen. This is a proportion of approximately one man to four tons of the ship's capacity. On this matter the statistics of earlier voyages are often faulty, but those we have suggest that in the sixteenth century long voyages had often started with one man to two tons, although they never finished with such a proportion. Improvements in the rig and gear of ships enabled the number of men to be reduced. In Cook's expedition, if we count the seamen alone, the proportion had come down to one man per five tons. Its significance lay not only in the longer endurance of the victuals but also in the better maintenance of cleanliness and preservation of health by avoiding overcrowding in the living quarters. Cook gave much thought to hygiene, and there is no doubt that his crew comprised not a man more than was necessary. He cannot have viewed with enthusiasm the influx of the large landsmen's party, which had grown to eleven from the eight for whom permission was originally sought. Five of the ship's company had been round the world with Wallis, and of these one, Lieutenant John Gore, had also served under Byron and was now starting on his third circumnavigation.

The tradition of long ocean voyages had hitherto been that scurvy was inevitable, and the salted food, lacking in what we have now learnt to call vitamins, was principally blamed. Seamen were well aware of the vitaminous principle in fresh food, although they had no scientific name for it. A good commander lost no opportunity of obtaining fresh meat, fruit and green vegetables, and of exchanging stale water for fresh. It had long been customary to carry live animals for slaughter as required, and experiments had already been made with unsalted portable soups and with fruit and vegetable juices. Cook used all these precautions, systematically and continuously, however much trouble they might entail upon himself and his men. But he did not rely solely on wholesome food. He believed, from his own observations, that scurvy and other diseases were bred by living quarters that were damp, uncleansed, and unventilated, by personal uncleanliness, and by insufficient clothing, causing men to neglect changing after getting wet and even to sleep in saturated garments. He therefore, as a matter of routine discipline, required all quarters to be regularly cleaned and ventilated whenever the weather permitted, and scrubbed with vinegar and fumigated at frequent intervals; and he insisted that his men should at all times be personally clean and well clothed. This policy was not to the taste of the generality, and there seems to have been some grumbling. But Cook enforced his orders, being quite determined that he would not have scurvy killing off his men, whatever might be their views on the subject. There was another aspect of this care for well-being that must have been more popular. It was that in normal circumstances Cook kept his crew on three watches, that is to say, each man had four hours on duty followed by eight hours off. The usual practice was to divide them into two watches, which meant four hours on and four hours off. It is not absolutely clear that the three-watch arrangement prevailed on this first expedition, but an entry in Cook's journal shows that it was in operation on the second, and it may very well have been part of his system from the outset.[1]

The *Endeavour* called at Madeira in order to take in wines at Funchal, these being a necessary part of the victualling. Neither water nor beer would keep good at sea for any length of time,

[1] Admiral J. R. Muir's *Cook*, p. 99, says that in the first voyage the crew were in three watches.

and the wines of Madeira and the Canaries were regularly used by long-distance voyagers. The course then lay almost south for Rio de Janeiro, another convenient refreshing point before quitting the bounds of civilization. On October 25 the ship crossed the equator, and the usual ducking ceremony was performed on those who had never been so far south before. It would be interesting to know when and with whom this ritual originated. There appears to be no mention of it in the writings of the Elizabethans, even in so detailed a description of sea life as the *Observations* of Sir Richard Hawkins. The victims were hauled up to the yardarm and let down three times into the sea. It was possible to escape by paying a forfeit in wine or spirits, and Banks and his party basely did so. Discipline forbade any idea of including the captain in Neptune's jurisdiction, although Cook himself had never crossed the line before.

At Rio de Janeiro the expedition met with an unpleasant reception from the Viceroy of Brazil. Portugal, like all other colonial powers, kept her colonial ports as the monopoly of her own shipping, and forbade access to the merchantmen of other countries. But international law, rudimentary as it was, had established an exception in favour of vessels in distress by reason of damage or want of victuals, and also of ships belonging to the governments of friendly nations. Great Britain and Portugal had been allies for more than a century, and Cook, as the commander of a King's ship, expected friendly treatment and full facilities. But the *Endeavour* did not look like a man-of-war and the Viceroy was deeply suspicious that she was engaged in clandestine trade. He declined even to look at Cook's commission in case it might be a fake. The explanation that the expedition was going to observe the transit of Venus had the same effect upon him as any claim to a moral or intellectual motive has upon an illiterate person whose mind moves only on the plane of material profit: he simply disbelieved it, and his suspicions were increased. He allowed watering and the purchase of victuals, under the supervision of an armed party of his own men. He allowed Cook to go on shore, but only in the company of a Portuguese officer who was to attend him everywhere. He refused to allow Banks or any of the others ashore even for the briefest visit. Cook finished his business and departed as soon as possible. He made energetic protests, but could not go farther in vindicating his position as the King's officer lest a delay should be caused which might imperil the appointment with Venus.

Perhaps for this reason Cook omitted to call at the Falkland Islands, where the British settlement still existed to afford facilities to Pacific-bound shipping. It will be remembered that Spain had already taken over the French claim to the islands. The resulting Falklands crisis and threat of war were destined to become acute in 1770, before Cook's return.

Sailing southwards from Rio out of sight of the land, the ship reached Tierra del Fuego on January 11, 1769. Cook's orders were to round Cape Horn, and not to pass through the Straits of Magellan, which from this time onwards were seldom used. He went through the Straits of Le Maire, between Tierra del Fuego and Le Maire's Staten Land, which was now known to be only a small island. Banks made a brief landing on it for botanical specimens while Cook wrote exact sailing directions for the passage of the Straits. Cape Horn itself lay to the south-west and had yet to be turned. It was a notorious region of bad weather, and Cook anchored in Success Bay to strike down his guns into the hold and make other preparations. Banks and his staff made an expedition into the country and were caught in a snowstorm. Although it was near midsummer the cold was so intense that two men were frozen to death and the others had a narrow escape. Cook was disappointed with the appearance of the natives, the alleged giants of so many travellers' tales. He found them to be of ordinary large build [1] and living in wretched conditions. It is curious how this story of the giants continued for nearly three centuries from Magellan's time. It must have

[1] "They are something above the middle size"—*Journal* (ed. Wharton), p. 37.

had a psychological element. Numerous European observers gave particulars of the gigantic stature of the men of the Straits and the adjacent country. Byron, to quote a late example, had said that they were eight feet high. But every now and again a man of sceptical mind had asserted that they were not abnormally tall. Cook was by no means the first of that opinion. It is of course possible that the believers and the sceptics had encountered different tribes. But where is the verifiable modern evidence for the eight-footers? They seem to have completely disappeared.

Good weather favoured the *Endeavour* as she rounded Cape Horn, without any of the struggle and setback so often experienced. After touching 60° S. Cook sailed in a generally north-west direction until he reached the parallel on which Tahiti would be found. This course took him well to the west of the tracks of Wallis, Carteret, and Bougainville, who had all kept closer to South America, and caused him to sail over a much larger area of Dalrymple's southern continent than they had done. In this long passage Cook perceived no signs of land except flights of birds at one point. This, as it turned out, was near Pitcairn Island, discovered by Carteret. Cook did not know of the discovery and did not see Pitcairn himself. Before reaching Tahiti the expedition sighted various lagoon islands but found no anchorage at any of them. At length, having reached the parallel of Tahiti, as recorded by Wallis, but at a point well to the eastward of Wallis's estimated longitude for the island, Cook "ran down the latitude" until Tahiti came in sight on April 10, 1769, in excellent time for the achievement of the first object of the undertaking.

The uncertainty of longitude was one of the factors in ocean navigation that was even then in process of elimination. Cook in these voyages played an accessory part in the change. Ever since the Renaissance it had been possible to determine latitudes with increasing accuracy by simple observations of the sun or a fixed star. Longitude had remained a more difficult and often insoluble problem. In practice it had depended on the dead reckoning or estimate of the distance made good, east or west of some fixed point, whose own longitudinal distance from the prime meridian might be by no means certain. The observation of eclipses, accurately carried out, yielded data for closer determination of longitude, but was rarely possible at sea. Theoretically the means of regularly ascertaining longitude was perfectly well known. It consisted in carrying on board ship a clock which would accurately preserve the time at the prime meridian, the difference between that time and the time at the point where the ship actually lay yielding the basis of a calculation of the number of degrees east or west of the prime meridian. But the difficulty was to construct such a clock, and centuries elapsed before it was overcome. Early in the eighteenth century the government of Queen Anne offered a reward of £20,000 for the discovery of a means of obtaining longitude within a prescribed degree of accuracy, and set up the Board of Longitude to investigate claims.

After fifty years John Harrison, a carpenter, produced the required timepiece by a miracle of craftsmanship. His chronometer, it was found, would preserve Greenwich time with the necessary accuracy on an ocean voyage. The Board of Longitude was somewhat loath to admit that the problem was solved (and so perhaps to terminate its own existence), and the personal intervention of George III was necessary to make it pay over the full reward. The story of his kindly interest, his summoning the inventor to a royal interview, and his, "Harrison, I'll see you righted!" sheds a pleasant gleam of light upon a much-abused king. All this was in progress but not finished when Cook sailed. The fact was not fully admitted that the chronometer had solved the problem, and only two or three chronometers as yet existed. So Cook went on his first Pacific voyage without one.

But Cook's fellow-observer was Charles Green, assistant to Nevil Maskelyne, the Astronomer Royal, who had recently perfected an astronomical method of finding Greenwich time and so solving the problem of longitude. Greenwich Observatory had long been working on this method, which consisted in measuring with a sextant the angular distance between the moon and some conspicuous star, and then finding from the new *Nautical Almanac* (first issued in 1767) at what instant by Greenwich time the two bodies were that distance apart.[1] The "lunar distance" method required great skill and entailed laborious calculations, but until chronometers became reliable it was the only good means of finding longitude. Cook learned the method from Green and was able by its means to record his discoveries with less than one degree of longitudinal inaccuracy.

Cook's expedition was at Tahiti more than seven weeks before the date of the transit and was destined to remain at the island for more than three months. Neither Wallis nor Bougainville had stayed so long, and neither of them had had so much business on shore as Cook's people had necessarily to undertake. The *Endeavour* expedition therefore underwent a searching test in the ability to deal successfully with high-spirited, friendly, but difficult natives whose code of conduct differed seriously from that of Europeans. On the whole the *Endeavour*'s people passed the test with honours, a result due to their own discipline and the leadership of Cook, aided by the tolerance with which Banks viewed all men, and the cheerful humour which he infused into all transactions. The stay at Tahiti

[1] See Commander Gould's *Cook*, pp. 47–50.

showed the practical civilization of the eighteenth century at its best. The whole story affords a strong contrast to the record of the Spaniards in Pacific islands in the sixteenth century. Leaders like Mendaña and Quiros had been full of benevolence towards the natives, but the outcome had always been bloodshed and misery. The sixteenth century lacked the sort of imagination which could compass the validity of other ways of life and other codes of ethics than the white man's. The highest benefit it could confer upon the islander was to lead him, summarily and without any patience, to give up behaving like a native and to imitate a European. Naturally the native did not understand, any more than he was understood, and the result was tragedy. The eighteenth century, in the persons of Cook and his company, approached the question with a radically different mentality. Religion had a good deal to do with it. The sixteenth century was fervent and bigoted, the eighteenth kept its beliefs very much to itself. The *Endeavour* did not even carry a chaplain. Quiros had had a dozen.

The *Endeavour* came to an anchor in Matavai Bay on the northernmost stretch of Tahiti's coastline. Swarms of the inhabitants came out in canoes and soon recognized Lieutenants Hicks and Gore and Robert Molyneux, the master, whom they had known during Wallis's visit two years before. All were friendly but excited, and

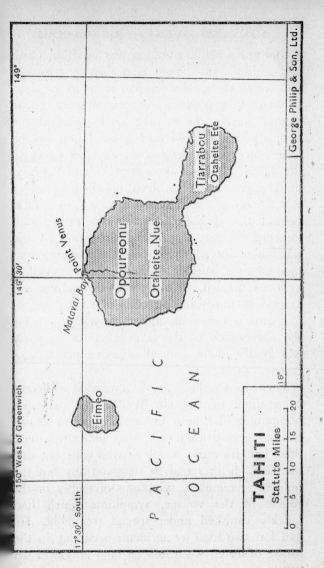

George Philip & Son, Ltd.

149°

149° 30'

Point Venus

Matavai Bay

Opoureonu

Otaheite-Nue

Tiarrabou

Otaheite Ete

150° West of Greenwich

Eimeo

P A C I F I C

O C E A N

17° 30' South

18°

TAHITI
Statute Miles

0     5     10     15     20

115

a cool grasp of the situation was needful. Cook and Banks went ashore next day to return a visit which the local chiefs had made to the ship. In view of the possibility that the situation might change during the coming weeks, and of the necessity that the scientific work should not be interrupted, Cook determined to build a fort on the shore. He chose the eastern side of the bay, at a place which involved no disturbance of native interests, and erected a strong earthwork, palisaded on its more accessible side, armed with some of the ship's guns and supported by the remainder, for which purpose the *Endeavour* was moored at a suitable distance. At Fort Venus, as it was named, all trade with the natives was carried on under the direction of Banks, and in due time the scientific apparatus was set up for the observation of the transit. A strong party was posted there and all military precautions taken.

These proceedings were somewhat different from those of Captain Wallis. His principal occupation had been the restoration to health of his scurvy-stricken sick, who comprised more than half his crew. Cook arrived with not one man sick, neither had he observed any but the mildest premonitory symptoms of scurvy in the course of the voyage, symptoms which had quickly vanished under special treatment. He had lost two men by accidents occurring in the course of duty, two frozen on land at Tierra del

Fuego, and one, a marine, by suicide. Soon after reaching Tahiti the artist Buchan died in an epileptic fit. Cook had the body taken out to sea for burial lest the British ceremony should offend the religious feelings of the Tahitians. It was the eighteenth-century attitude again. One can imagine how the sixteenth would have made it an occasion for impressing the heathen.

Banks was not only a botanist but a man of universal curiosity. To him the Tahitians were a study of first-class interest, from the pretty girl with a fire in her eyes to the grizzled chiefs whose authority over their vivacious subjects seemed at times to be very ineffective. Tahitian society was like a large school under go-as-you-please discipline, in which there was no real vice but a great deal of noise and disorder. Banks threw himself into it with zest, made social excursions, attended banquets, traded ship's stores for pigs and fruit, and followed up native thieves of British property like a terrier after a rat.

Theft provided the chief difference of opinion between hosts and guests and the chief source of uneasiness lest the good relations should break down. Expert thieving ("prodigious expert," Cook called it) was the Tahitian national pastime. It had little of the meanness of white men's stealing, but was pursued rather as a mischievous sport than a path to gain. The interest lay rather in the skilful conveyance and baffling of pursuit than in the value of the objects stolen, which were sometimes recovered without much difficulty when the thieves had won their game. Like sportsmen also, the Tahitians were prepared to take punishment when they failed, and showed little resentment when the British exacted it. While guests at a feast and concert some of the British party had their pockets picked. Cook's stockings were stolen from under his head while he lay asleep, or, as he claimed, awake. At the gate of the fort some natives hustled the sentry, snatched his musket, and ran off with it. The guard fired and killed the chief culprit. This might have been the dividing action between friendship and war, and for some hours not a native came near the fort. But at length they decided that the victim's death was on his own head and that the British were justified in stopping him by any means in their power. The most serious theft occurred when the scientific apparatus had been landed. The quadrant, still packed in its case, was carried off by night in spite of the sentries' vigilance. Banks and Green and a midshipman went in pursuit immediately the loss was discovered. Cook followed with an armed party, and made the chiefs understand that this time there must be no nonsense. The culprits were obliged to restore the quadrant. They had already taken it out of its box and distributed some of the parts. All were eventually recovered, but the health of the instrument was not improved and was subsequently blamed by Cook for some inaccuracy in the observations.

At length the great day arrived, hot and cloudless, ideal for the work in hand. Cook and Green observed every phase of the transit at Fort Venus, while two other parties, spaced out in case of local obscuration, observed from points many miles away on either side. Locally the programme was achieved with complete success, but the outcome of the whole enterprise was failure. An unforeseen optical distortion vitiated all the readings obtained both in the Pacific and at the North Cape and Hudson Bay, and no accurate or even approximate calculation of the sun's distance could be obtained from them.[1] In fact, it seems that, even with this source of error removed, the observation of the transit is not a method capable of yielding a good solution of the problem, which has been solved by other means.

The building of Fort Venus and preparation for the scientific work had hitherto occupied all energies. It was now necessary to prepare for exploration in unknown and tempestuous seas, and a thorough overhaul and refit of the *Endeavour* had to be carried out. While it was in progress Cook attended to his own especial duty by sailing round the island in the pinnace and making a careful survey of the coast. With his strong interest in hygiene he was troubled by

[1] Commander Gould is the first of Cook's biographers to go into the question of the success of the observations.

the fact that although scurvy had spared his crew, venereal disease had not. Numerous cases developed during the stay at Tahiti. Cook believed that the natives had been free from infection before the coming of the white men, and he laid the blame on Bougainville's Frenchmen. He exonerated Wallis's English because their captain's log made no mention of any such thing at Tahiti, and he was also convinced that the *Endeavour* was free from disease when she arrived there. When the evil became apparent he did his best to prevent intercourse, but was unsuccessful. It was a matter beyond the scope of naval discipline. On the day of the transit some of the men took advantage of the officers' preoccupation to break into the trading stores and help themselves to nails, which were the established currency in Tahiti. On detecting one man with nails in his possession, Cook awarded him two dozen lashes, the severest punishment recorded in the voyage. But it was all of no avail, and the mutual defilement of white men and natives continued. When the day of sailing drew near two marines absented themselves, intending to remain among the natives, who were quite ready to receive them. But Cook was determined to recapture them at all costs, and did so; and they also received two dozen. Several Tahitians, on their side, were anxious to take passage in the *Endeavour*. Cook accepted a chief named Tupia, having made him understand that there could be no guarantee of his return.

In mid-July, when Cook quitted Tahiti, it was winter in the southern latitudes which he had to search. He therefore spent a month in examining the islands which the Tahitians reported to the north-westward, and which he called the Society group. Tupia, who had been born in one of these islands, was a useful guide and interpreter. He was an intelligent man, who knew that there were many more islands than those in the vicinity, but he knew nothing of any continental land. In mid-August, with the crew somewhat recovered from the dissipations of Tahiti, Cook sailed southwards to look for *Terra Australis* according to his instructions. He pressed on for a fortnight until he reached 40° S. amid increasingly bad weather which took its toll of sails and gear. It was as far as he had been ordered to go. No land was seen, and the large swell rolling up from the southward showed that no land of any size existed for a long distance on. *Terra Australis Incognita* did not include any attractive latitude in this part of the Pacific. That did not prove that it was entirely a fable, for vast untraversed areas still remained.

The next instruction enjoined Cook to sail westwards, as far as possible in 40° S., until he should come to Tasman's New Zealand, of which land he was to determine the nature and connexions. Tasman had seen only the western side of New Zealand. Having coasted northward after sighting it, he was able to believe that it was a projection of the great continent. Had he rounded it by the south, he would have learned his mistake. Cook's course would lead to the eastern and unknown side of New Zealand. He was not able to keep along the fortieth parallel in approaching it, as the winds forced him to the northwards, but he was able to make most of the course south of 35°. After five weeks he sighted the east coast of New Zealand just short of 39° S. Here at last, after long sailing over a hypothetical continent, was something solid but as yet amorphous. The next six months of work done in the characteristically Cook style were to give it a very definite shape indeed.

It was on October 7, 1769, that the boy Nick Young sighted the point which his captain thereupon named Young Nick's Head, and the exploration of the New Zealand coastline began. The point was an arm of Poverty Bay, near the middle of the eastern coast of North Island. Cook at first coasted southwards past Hawke Bay to Cape Turnagain, where he decided to reverse his direction and work round the northern end of the country. The Maori natives, although racially akin to the Tahitians and speaking the same language, were different in character. They were hostile and unabashed, having no instinctive feeling of inferiority to the strange newcomers. They came out in canoes to inspect the ship, would sometimes trade on the principle traditionally assigned to the Dutch, of "giving too little and asking too much," and threw stones and other missiles with small provocation. Firing over their heads did not impress them, as Cook found on a painful occasion. He tried to stop a canoe by this method in order to obtain information. Its occupants reacted violently, and the English had to shoot to kill in order to save their own lives. Four Maoris were slain. Cook was much perturbed. He had meant no harm, but the tragedy had resulted from his mistaken action. In the later stages of the exploration relations with the tribesmen became easier as experience was gained in dealing with them. But New Zealand never offered the carefree hospitality of Tahiti. Murderous violence was always ready to break out.

Cook proceeded slowly enough to make an accurate record of the salient points and the trend of the coastline. In this way he reached and turned the northern point, which Tasman had named Cape Maria Van Diemen, before the end of 1769. He then went south along the western coast charted by Tasman until he came to the great opening between the two main islands of New Zealand. Tasman had laid this down as a bay, although he suspected that it might be a strait. Cook proved it to be a strait and sailed through it, and it has been known as Cook Strait thenceforward. Before passing through, he stayed for a month and careened the ship in order to clean her of a growth of weed and barnacles at a sheltered inlet which he named Queen Charlotte's Sound. It became a regular port for refreshment and refit in subsequent voyages. He had now almost circumnavigated the North Island and was fairly sure that it had no continental connexion. There was, however, a gap of a hundred miles from Cook Strait to Cape Turnagain from which he had begun the northward survey. To remove all doubt he coasted this unknown stretch, approached and identified Cape Turnagain from the opposite side to that which he had quitted, and then turned south to investigate what lay beyond Cook Strait. Here if anywhere was the continental possibility. Close and determined coasting would reveal the truth.

Still methodically surveying, Cook passed slowly down the east coast of the South Island, making progress only in the daytime and avoiding running into danger at night by standing on and off in the water already reached. In this way he missed none of the salient features of the coast. But he was often several miles distant from it and did not see the entrances to all the inlets. Distance caused him to see the extensive Banks Peninsula as an island, just as, on the English coast, Beachy Head sometimes appears as an island to observers sailing up Channel from the west; and later, at the far southern extremity, he

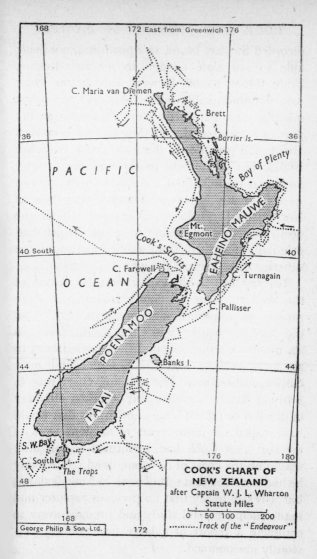

168  172 East from Greenwich 176

C. Maria van Diemen

C. Brett

36  Barrier Is. 36

P A C I F I C

Bay of Plenty

Mt. Egmont

40 South 40

O C E A N

C. Farewell

EAHEINO MAUWE

Cook's Straits

C. Turnagain

C. Pallisser

POENAMOO

44 Banks I. 44

TAVAI

S.W. Bay

176 180

C. South

The Traps

48

**COOK'S CHART OF
NEW ZEALAND**
after Captain W. J. L. Wharton
Statute Miles

0 50 100 200

.......... *Track of the "Endeavour"*

168 172

George Philip & Son, Ltd.

C.O.P.—5*

recorded Stewart Island as a peninsula, not being able to sail close enough to see the dividing strait. Once round Stewart Island, the coast turned unmistakably northward, and the prime question was answered: New Zealand was not part of a great continent. Maoris had been seen about half-way down the east coast of South Island, but from there to the end the country appeared uninhabited. The southern natives were in many ways less advanced than those of North Island. Owing to its warmer climate the north was more desirable to a race which had originally migrated from the tropics, and the superior tribes pushed the inferior southwards.

The last link in the exploration, the survey of the western coast of South Island, was more rapidly accomplished, and on March 27, 1770, the *Endeavour* was back in Cook Strait, having in six months circumnavigated the North Island in an anti-clockwise and the South Island in a clockwise direction. The resulting chart was, as a broad sketch, complete and accurate, although in detail it could not hope to be so; for that would have called for many years of arduous work of the sort that Cook had performed season after season on the coast of Newfoundland. Obviously he had not done that sort of work in New Zealand; but it is safe to say that no previous explorer had made such a careful study and brought away so complete a report of a large new country previously unexamined.

## Chapter Six

# The First Voyage : New South Wales

WITH the exploration of New Zealand, Cook had fulfilled the Admiralty's instructions, except the last, which was to return to England by any route he thought fit. There were two directions in which he might sail—east by Cape Horn, and west by the Cape of Good Hope. The Cape Horn route offered the certainty of virtually settling the question of the existence of the now diminished southern continent. By sailing from the longitude of New Zealand to that of Tierra del Fuego in a far southerly latitude, 50 degrees or higher, the track would pass through seas never before traversed. If the voyagers found the ocean open and empty, as Cook expected they would, it would be the end of the continental possibility considered in its economical and political aspect. Nothing south of that would have any bearing on national policy, since, latitude for latitude, the South Pacific was a good deal colder than the North Atlantic, and anything beyond fifty degrees would be as barren and repellent as the Falklands and Tierra del Fuego. The bleak and treeless Falklands are the same distance from the equator as the Isle of Wight. If, on the other hand, the course revealed land, it could be rounded by the north and its general outline determined. The wind was favourable to the Cape Horn passage, for in the higher latitudes it blew almost continuously from the west.

In spite of its attractions Cook decided against the Cape Horn route. After eighteen months at sea the ship's hull was needing dockyard attention, and her sails and gear were wearing out. Provisions for four months were still in hand, which left no great margin for a voyage through a part of the world where many unpredictable casualties might occur and no supplies would be obtainable. It was now April, and the southern winter about to begin. The probable winds, though fair, would be very strong, and the *Endeavour* might expect to run for thousands of miles before an almost continuous gale, with many more hours of darkness than of daylight in which to strike an unknown coast. On the whole Cook thought it was not a fair venture and concluded that the high latitudes must be left to a subsequent voyage.

The Cape route offered a passage in kindlier regions, with a refit and supplies of necessaries at Batavia on the way. It offered also a piece of new discovery which had needed doing for over a century, the finding and investigation of eastern Australia. Many explorers had been drawn to the task and had shirked closing with it. Bougainville had come nearest, but even he had turned away. All of them had reached the scene with their ships more or less decayed and their crews ravaged by scurvy. Cook's *Endeavour*, although the worse for wear, was by no means in decay, and his men were fit as none had ever been in those seas before. He determined to find the east coast of Australia and to explore it from south to north, and then to seek Batavia by way of Torres Strait (vouched for by Dalrymple) if it should be found to exist; if not, to go round the eastern end of New Guinea as all previous voyagers (except the doubtfully attested Torres) had done.

We have seen how the Dutch had coasted and placed on cartographic record all western Australia, the south coast for about half its length, and rather more of the north coast, including the whole circuit of the Gulf of Carpentaria. In sum the Dutch captains had compiled a continuous outline of about half of the Australian continent. Besides this, Tasman had discovered the west, south, and east coasts of what is now named Tasmania, but he had not found whether it was a separate land or a part of Australia. The nature, shape, and connexions of eastern Australia were all to seek. No European was known ever to have seen it. Nearly everyone supposed it to be continuous with New Guinea.

It might be continuous with Tasman's Van Diemen's Land. Some even imagined that it stretched out in a great bulge north-eastwards to form the continent that Quiros was believed to have seen. Bougainville had indeed disproved that, but Cook knew nothing of Bougainville, who had not come home when the *Endeavour* left Europe. With a worn ship and a good crew, and four months' victuals which he could stretch to six, Cook sailed to his greatest discovery, New South Wales. He left New Zealand on April 1, 1770.

Cook intended to sight Van Diemen's Land and pick up the discovery of its coastline at the point where Tasman had left it. Thus, going northwards, he would determine the nature of Van Diemen's Land, whether insular or continental, and would proceed up the eastern coast of Australia. The name Australia, it should be mentioned, is here used for convenience, but did not then exist. The country was universally called New Holland until the early years of the nineteenth century, when the word Australia, proposed by the explorer Matthew Flinders, came gradually into use and was officially adopted in 1817. Bad weather interfered with Cook's intention. When he was nearing Van Diemen's Land a southerly gale forced him out of his course, and on April 21 the *Endeavour* came in sight of Point Hicks on the Australian mainland. Cook therefore did not settle the question of the junction or separation of Van Diemen's Land. In his second voyage there was another opportunity of doing so, but again it was missed; and the discovery never was made until 1798, when Flinders, accompanied by George Bass, sailed through the channel since known as Bass's Strait and proved that Van Diemen's Land was an island.

Owing to his small remaining stock of victuals, Cook had not unlimited time to carry out his programme, and he decided to begin his northward coasting from the point first sighted. For the same reason his survey of the coast, although accurate to an extent achieved by no earlier explorer in laying down the general outline and the distances and directions between salient points, did not extend to an investigation of all inlets and harbours, most of which there was not time to enter.

For more than a week the *Endeavour* followed the new coast northwards, finding no harbour which would admit boats to the shore without danger from the surf. During that time a few natives were seen—"Indians," the explorers called them—and the country appeared moderately attractive to the distant observer. On the morning of April 29 a deeper indentation was discovered, ultimately to be named Botany Bay.[1] The pinnace reported a safe passage between

[1] Cook at first called it Stingray Harbour, from the abundance of those fish in its waters.

the enclosing heads and a good anchorage within; and later in the day the ship sailed into her first Australian port. Four natives, fishing in small canoes, took not the slightest notice of the unprecedented spectacle, and when they had made their catch took it ashore and cooked it and fed their families with complete unconcern. Others who had been seen by the boat party earlier in the day had been more demonstrative and had brandished spears and boomerangs. The latter weapon was new to the English, who described it as a short scimitar or curved sword.

Cook and Banks went ashore, taking two boats with armed crews. Two armed aborigines came down to the beach to oppose the landing. They shouted loudly and signed to the English to withdraw. Tupia the Tahitian was put forward to interpret as he had so usefully done in New Zealand. But these people understood not a word of his, nor he of theirs. The eighteenth century was facing prehistoric man, and neither quite grasped that it was opposed by something beyond its comprehension. For several minutes the deadlock continued, Cook ready to land with thirty disciplined men behind him, the two savages forty yards up the sandy beach threatening extremities against any advance. Signs of peace and offers of gifts being unavailing, Cook fired over the heads of the warriors, and still they did not retreat. Then he resorted to a charge of small shot, the distance precluding any danger of a fatal hit. After being peppered twice, one man ran away, but only to fetch a wooden shield with which he again faced the invaders. After two more terrifying discharges the patriots fled, but they had stood up more bravely than most would have done in their situation. The reason for their resistance soon appeared, for behind the beach among the trees were found their huts, containing children whom they had not been able to carry away. The English took some weapons and left as equivalent the usual toys and novelties coveted by savages. But later they found that these natives had shown no curiosity and had left the things untouched. They were altogether different from the active-minded islanders of New Zealand and Tahiti. Their canoes were the worst imaginable, roughly made of bark and useful only for fishing along the enclosed shore of the bay.

Cook's first object in landing was to obtain water. At first no good supply was apparent, but later streams were discovered on both the north and south sides of the bay. The explorers were greatly impressed with the excellence of the bay as a safe harbour. Such estimates are comparative. They had been coasting for several days without finding any anchorage, and the first one discovered appeared highly desirable. The permanent British occupants of the country who came later did not share that opinion, finding that the bay was not nearly so good as it looked. It was so shoal near shore that ships had to lie out in the middle, exposed to the sea that an easterly wind sent in between the heads. But Governor Arthur Phillip, who commanded the pioneer settlement, came with a frigate and a fleet of transports, individually larger vessels than Cook's little shallow-draught *Endeavour*; and Cook was not thinking in terms of frigates when he assessed the qualities of a new coastline.

Banks did as much land exploration as possible. He found himself in a naturalist's paradise and was almost overwhelmed by the mass of new specimens collected by himself and his following. But he did not appear to be impressed by the fertility of the country or its suitability as a place of settlement. "Reading his journal," says Professor Wood, "we get the impression that he thought Botany Bay to be a very good place for botanists, but a very bad place for colonists." It was Cook who left on record an opinion that was on the whole favourable, with mention of rich meadow land and soil fit for cultivation. Australians of the locality have never found this soil, and the reasons for Cook's estimate remain a mystery. He had worked on the land until he was seventeen, and should have known enough for a sound judgment. When the decision on the site of an Australian colony came to be made in 1787 Cook was dead, but the advice of Banks prevailed in favour of Botany Bay. He seemed to have forgotten his own early impressions and to have adopted with exaggeration those of Cook. Phillip duly sailed into Botany Bay in 1788, disliked both its land and its waters, and after a few days moved the settlement northwards to Port Jackson, the next break in the coastline, where he founded the city of Sydney.

To return to 1770, Cook, having watered at Botany Bay, sailed on May 7. He went slowly northward along the coast, as close as was prudent, carefully laying down the position of all points and noting the probable nature of inlets, but he did not anchor again for a fortnight. In this way he saw but did not enter the great inlet to which he gave the name Port Jackson, and passed and named other features of the coast-line which at this stage appeared attractive, with "hills, ridges and valleys, and large plains all clothed with woods." With further north-ward progress the pleasing aspect deteriorated and the land became barren and repellent. On the 17th Cook examined and named, without stopping, Moreton Bay, on which the city of Brisbane was afterwards to arise. He was now north of the modern New South Wales and coast-ing Queensland. On the 23rd he anchored in Bustard Bay, whose only recommendation was that it provided an excellent meal with a specimen of the bird from which it received its name. Shortly after leaving this anchorage the *Endeavour* crossed the tropic of Capricorn, having already coasted over a thousand miles.

Hitherto the exploration had been easy, but difficulties now began to appear, and soon the navigation became fantastically dangerous. North of Bustard Bay the coastline is obstructed by shoals, and it was no longer possible to keep as close to the land as Cook would have wished. Far out to sea, between one and two hundred miles from the coast, was something else of which he knew nothing, the southern end of the Great Barrier Reef. This mass of coral formations, rising sheer from the depth of the ocean, runs north-westwards, not quite parallel to the Queensland coast, but converging steadily upon it. The gap between reef and mainland is thus widest at the southern end, and for some distance in there is comparatively clear sailing water. But as the main reef draws nearer to the land the intervening sea becomes obstructed by innumerable smaller coral reefs and islands, scattered without plan and forming a maze of dangers and barriers. The great reef, like a great mountain range, is an area rather than a line, but on its north-eastern side, fronting the open Pacific, it does present more of a linear aspect than can be discerned in the jumble between it and the Queensland shore. But even on the ocean side there are separate outliers, and the main reef is pierced by gaps through which the tide pours fiercely. Bougainville had approached the Barrier Reef from the eastward and had drawn back before getting too deeply

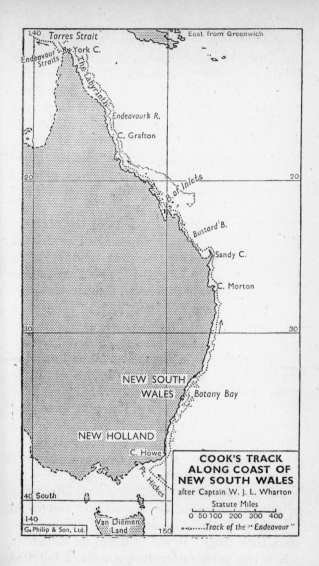

COOK'S TRACK
ALONG COAST OF
NEW SOUTH WALES
after Captain W. J. L. Wharton

Statute Miles

0 50 100 200 300 400

••••• *Track of the "Endeavour"*

involved. His experience, and the very existence of the reef, were unknown to Cook, who sailed in from the southwards between the barrier and the land and became involved in a thickening tangle of dangers as he pressed forward. He had no thought of turning back and getting out by the way he had come in. He was intent on tracing the coastline and settling the question of the existence of Torres Strait. Forward it had to be.

Keeping as close to the land as the obstacles permitted, Cook sailed slowly northward, with leadsmen continually sounding and look-outs vigilant aloft. On June 11 the soundings became irregular, alternating between shallow and deep as the ship passed over steep hills of coral rising from the sea floor. At night an area of deeper water seemed to have been reached. There was a smooth sea and a bright moon, and instead of anchoring Cook sailed forward with canvas so reduced that the ship's speed was only one knot. He was taking advantage of fine weather to edge cautiously towards safer water, not knowing that the reef-strewn area here extended for fifty miles to the nearest part of the open ocean. Between 10 and 11 p.m. there were soundings showing from ten to twenty fathoms, the last being seventeen; and then, before another cast could be made, the *Endeavour* struck and remained fast on a coral ledge. It was in the exact latitude in which two years earlier Bougainville, a hundred and fifty miles out to sea, had turned away from the outlying reefs.

On board the *Endeavour* the behaviour of every man was exemplary. Cook grasped immediate control over the situation, his cool brain thinking two or three moves ahead of the phase actually in progress. Only so could effort be faultlessly applied, without the doing and undoing, the counter-order and recrimination, that show a commander to be rattled. The officers reflected his demeanour, and the men worked quietly and steadfastly without any blasphemy or excitement. Banks was astonished, for he had heard that it was customary in case of shipwreck for the sailors to refuse all command and get drunk. He and the other landsmen, "the gentlemen," as Cook calls them, merited and received their captain's commendation for zeal and absence of panic. And so every hand and mind were bent to the saving of the ship.

There was a procedure for such occasions built up through centuries of experience: to get all sail off the ship, hoist out the boats and take soundings all round to find out the lie of the reef and the deep water; then to get anchors out in the direction which offered the best chance of hauling off, and heave taut on the cables; meanwhile to lighten the ship by every possible means, striking down spars and letting them float overboard, and getting up from the hold all articles that could be dispensed with and throwing them into the sea. Cook sacrificed in this way some condemned stores, thirty tons of fresh water, a quantity of firewood, much stone and iron ballast, and six guns from the main deck. The *Endeavour* had struck at the top of high water, and the measures described above took hours to execute. Meanwhile the tide was falling. The difference between high and low water on this coast was only four feet, but that was more than enough to nullify all the lightening measures until the tide should again rise. When it did so near midday it was a disappointment. In spite of her loss of displacement no heaving on all the cables would budge the ship. The day tides hereabouts do not rise so high as the night tides, and another long wait was necessitated. But the next night tide did its business handsomely. Well before high water the ship floated free, to be hauled clear and anchored in deep water while the spars were replaced and preparations made for sailing away.

The moment of getting off the reef was crucial, for the next few minutes would probably answer the question, would she float or would she sink without the rocks to support her? All knew that she was holed, but how badly remained to be seen. It was found that she was taking in a lot of water, but that the pumps could just deal with it at the cost of exhausting labour. A great improvement was then effected by the operation of fothering, the hauling under the damaged bottom of a sail to which quantities of wool and oakum were loosely attached. This material was sucked into the leaks and went far to stop them, after which the water was kept down by a single pump. But this was the most temporary of makeshifts, and it was essential to find some spot where the *Endeavour* could be beached and patched up. By good fortune the weather was calm. If it had been otherwise, the ship would have gone to pieces on the reef or sunk after getting off. Probably not one of her company would have seen England again. No other ship came that way for the rest of the eighteenth century.

As soon as it was light Cook sent away the boats to search for a harbour. They found a river—now Endeavour River—in latitude $15\frac{1}{2}°$ S., with a narrow entrance and depth enough within for the ship to float close to the shore. Thither Cook sailed her, finding just enough water to pass over the bar with nothing to spare. No ship-of-war or ordinary merchantman could have been taken in, and indeed the whole story of this dangerous Australian exploration formed a vindication of the choice of a shallow-draught collier. Any vessel not built to take the ground habitually and stand hard pounding might well have received fatal injury on the coral reef. The river was a secure haven for the tasks to be performed. The first was to bring the ship within twenty feet of the beach and take everything out of her fore part, forming a camp on shore in which some of the men could live. Thus lightened, it was possible to haul her so far up the beach on a high tide that the injured part was exposed when the water fell. There were several holes where the sharp coral had pierced the planking, but the largest was filled by a piece which had broken off. The carpenters made as strong a repair as they could, but it was only superficial, and it was not possible even to ascertain the full extent of the damage. A good deal of the outer sheathing had been torn off the hull, leaving the structure exposed to the ravages of the tropical worm. Altogether it was advisable to seek a dockyard without delay, and the nearest was at Batavia in the Dutch East Indies.

All this took more than six weeks, and it was not until August 6 that Cook was able to sail out of the river. In the meantime the naturalists had been investigating fauna and flora hitherto unknown. Among the animals the dingo and the kangaroo were encountered for the first time, while a sailor reported meeting a being which he conceived to be the Devil and refrained from challenging. Modern commentators have variously interpreted his description as indicating a flying fox or a wallaby. Contact with the natives was made for the first time since Botany Bay. They were a little more communicative than the earlier acquaintances, but their way of thought were hard to follow. When the demanded and were refused a turtle which the white men caught on the reef, they considered themselves unjustly treated and started a bush fire which endangered the camp.

The Endeavour River is about half-way along the eastern side of the northward projection of Queensland, which narrows to the point of Cape York about four and a half degrees farther north. Cook did not know with certainty that he was coasting a peninsula whose other side formed the shore of the Gulf of Carpentaria, neither was he by any means certain that there was a channel between northern Australia and southern New Guinea. The old Spanish document on the voyage of Torres, communicated by Dalrymple to Banks, said that a strait existed. The explorations of various Dutchmen, including Tasman himself, in the Gulf of Carpentaria, had produced the opposite conclusion. The Dutch were unanimous that there was no strait and that continuous land linked New Holland and New Guinea. Historical documents were not Cook's own field of discovery, and after sailing over huge areas of Dalrymple's southern continent he could not have implicit faith in that investigator's judgment. Yet he thought the possibility of the strait sufficiently good to be worth following up. It was one of the jobs that needed to be done, and if the result were favourable it would yield the shortest passage to Batavia. He determined to make for the strait.

Outside to the northward the shoals and islets became thicker than ever, and a strong breeze compelled Cook to anchor because it made the ship go dangerously fast. He decided at length to get right outside the area of the reefs, even though this meant losing sight of the Australian shore. There were now three pressing reasons for haste towards Batavia: the ship was damaged and still leaking, the victuals were running low, and in November the north-west monsoon was due to set in, which would be a foul wind causing an interminable prolongation of the passage. Cook therefore got out into clear water and sailed comfortably for three days, the first spell for over a thousand miles in which the *Endeavour* had moved without a leadsman continuously on duty. The penalty of those three days was a blank space in Cook's outline of the Australian coast. On the third day something happened to restore contact. As the ship skirted at a respectful distance the outer side of the main reef the wind died completely away. A great swell from the open ocean was breaking on the reef, and this swell carried the helpless vessel irresistibly towards destruction. Here there would be no kedging off, but a quick dissolution under the battering of the great hills of water that burst upon the coral. This outer wall rose sheer from the ocean floor, and a sounding showed that no anchor would reach bottom at the fullest scope of the cable. Cook ordered out the boats to tow, but the effect was insufficient and the reef came closer. A small opening appeared, through which the ebb tide was gushing out. Its stream aided the boats to get the *Endeavour* farther from the danger. Then a light air stirred the sails and hope increased. Later, when the tide was flowing, Cook saw another opening and determined to pass within. He had had enough of sailing outside the Great Barrier Reef. "It is but a few days ago," he wrote, "that I rejoiced at having got without the reef, but that joy was nothing when compared with what I now felt at being safe at an anchor within it."

He closed the shore as far as possible, and the chart once more takes up its tale and continues to the tip of Cape York. On August 21, 1770, Cook knew that he had reached the end of the long, dangerous coast of eastern Australia. The main shore ceased to stretch northwards, where islands and water channels took its place and, a sign of certainty, round the extremity came a swell from the south-west. There was open water to the westward, and there was a strait between Australia and New Guinea. Cook knew that he was not its first discoverer, and took credit for no more than settling a doubtful point; and the strait as a whole has justly received the name of Torres. But Torres had passed along the New Guinea side and had not seen Australia. Cook found a route, through the usual maze of obstacles, between Cape York and its outlying islands, and this passage is called Endeavour Strait. Before leaving, he landed and took formal possession of the whole east coast to which he had stuck so closely. If ever a pioneer had the right to make such a claim for his country it was he. For the exploration had been in a new manner, the Cook manner, such as no first-beholder of a new coastline had ever practised since geography began. Certainly no eighteenth-century captain, from Bougainville backwards, had exhibited method, skill, forethought, and determination in the same high degree.

Cook's life-story is so straightforward and devoid of mysteries as to afford little scope to writers who delight in reconstructing "the truth about A. B." or "the hidden story of the X expedition." Such would be hard put to it to find anything piquant in Cook's record. But this Australian exploration has provided two meagre little problems of nomenclature about which, in default of anything more exciting, some discussion has been carried on: why and when did Cook alter Stingray Harbour to Botany Bay?—and: when did he bestow the name New South Wales? Nothing in the least important depends on the answers to these questions.

Of a different kind was an attempt made by Alexander Dalrymple to impugn Cook's candour. In the first chapter of this book reference was made to the French maps of the period 1530–50 which suggest that some discovery of eastern

Australia had then been made. On what may be taken for Cook's coast certain of these maps bear two inscriptions, *Coste des herbaiges* and *Coste dangereuse*. The first is in the vicinity of Botany Bay, and it signifies simply that the adjacent country is green and open, neither forested nor arid. The words *Coste dangereuse* are extended along the line of what we now know to be the Great Barrier Reef; and unless we are to believe in an improbable coincidence, they do seem to show that someone had been there before 1530. But at the time of Cook's voyage these maps were lying in oblivion. Dalrymple himself did not know of their existence, neither did any other writer on South Sea discovery. Afterwards some person who perceived that Cook's discovery had lent a new interest to one of these unregarded maps drew Banks's attention to it. Banks bought the map, kept it for some time, and ultimately presented it to the British Museum. Dalrymple, whose resentment against Cook was undying, fastened on it like a leech. He declared that Cook must have seen the map before making his voyage, and knew that he was not the first discoverer; and had claimed nevertheless that he was. At the time of this puerile accusation Cook was dead and unable to defend himself. To any reasonable mind he needs no defence.

After passing the straits Cook crossed over to the southern side of New Guinea and took his way westward to the Dutch Indies. He obtained victuals at Savu and reached Batavia on October 10, 1770. He naturally did not disclose to the Dutch the nature of his voyage, although no doubt much of it leaked out during the three months' contact of his whole crew with the people of Batavia; and he obtained without trouble the usual facilities for repair and refit. He forwarded to the Admiralty by a homeward-bound Dutch ship a full account of the voyage, and was able to claim that he had not lost one man by scurvy. The ship needed extensive repairs, for the damage sustained on the coral reef proved to be much more serious than had been supposed. It was this that occasioned the long stay at Batavia and the deaths of many good men who should have lived to tell the tale of the voyage. For Batavia, with its malaria and dysentery, was "the land that kills." Although common sense and experience could overcome a deficiency disease like scurvy, something more, beyond the ken of the eighteenth century, was needed to defeat malignant bacteria. The *Endeavour's* company began to die, and when at length they got clear from the fatal port they carried death with them all the way to the Cape of Good Hope, where at length in the pure South African air some improvement took place. Charles Green the astronomer died, as did Hicks the lieutenant and Molyneux the master, Monkhouse the surgeon, and Tupia the Tahitian adventurer who had taken passage to see the world. Altogether thirty men succumbed in the post-Batavian section of the voyage. Eight had been lost, mostly by accident, in the course of exploration. The *Endeavour* had sailed with ninety-four on board, and she brought home fifty-six. Three of the survivors were commissioned on Cook's recommendation: Charles Clerke, who had been a midshipman and afterwards an A.B. and had passed his examination for lieutenant; Richard Pickersgill, who succeeded Molyneux as master; and John Edgecumbe, the sergeant of marines.

It was a defect inherent in her good qualities that the *Endeavour* was not a fast sailer, and the final passage from the Cape to England took three months. On July 10, 1771, Cook had sight of the English coast. He sailed up Channel and anchored in the Downs on the 12th.

*Chapter Seven*

# The Second Voyage

THE results of Cook's first voyage were of interest to the Royal Society, the Admiralty, and the intelligent public. For the last-mentioned a voluminous account by Dr. John Hawkesworth was published. It was based upon material from the journals of Cook and Banks, but it contained some absurd and nonsensical statements of which neither of them would have been guilty. The guise in which it was put forward made it seem that Cook was responsible, and he felt that he had been badly treated. His own journal, to us infinitely preferable, was thought unsuitable for lack of polish. The eighteenth century held that a literary gentleman was indispensable to the writing of a book which should adequately adorn a great subject. The journal was not published until 1893.

To the Royal Society were handed all the observations of the transit taken at Tahiti. It had also those obtained at the northern stations. For reasons already mentioned the total result was so unsatisfactory as to amount to failure. The Astronomer Royal, in commenting on the readings, remarked that those taken by Charles

Green betrayed a lack of care or skill. Cook retorted that Green's book of observations contained the whole of his readings, written down in pencil as he took them, and that his death had taken place before he had fair-copied them with the omission of those that were discordant. Evidently this was the accepted scientific practice in the eighteenth century. Presumably it is not now. It obviously created a temptation to show a result having a smoothness not warranted by the facts.

For the Admiralty and for British statesmen in general the chief interest was in new coastlines, not only those of New Zealand, New South Wales, and Torres Strait, but those which might exist but had not yet been seen. The great southern continent remained the dominating factor in Pacific policy. Cook's voyage had lopped off large tracts of it, but disturbing possibilities remained. During his absence the crisis of 1770 had almost produced another maritime war with the Bourbon powers; and the bone of contention had been the possession of the Falkland Islands, valueless in themselves, but desirable as a base for the coming exploitation of the South Pacific. Great Britain was willing to fight for the Falklands. Spain was willing to fight with the assistance of France. The French seemed almost willing, but at the pinch their nerve failed. The Bourbon powers gave way and left the British in possession of what turned out to be a barren conquest. But it was barren only because the South Seas were barren of populous and civilized continents; and in 1770 no one knew the truth of that.

In 1771 Cook could reveal only a portion of the truth. Another voyage was needed to discover the rest. Meanwhile the French were keenly at work, and even the Spaniards made a show of energy in the ocean which had once been theirs and whose monopoly they still claimed. As early as 1739 Lozier Bouvet had discovered what he supposed to be continental land in the far South Atlantic and had named it Cape Circumcision. He recorded its position inaccurately, and the island (for such it was) could be positively identified only in the late nineteenth century. It is now called Bouvet Island. In Cook's time Bougainville's voyage inaugurated a whole series of French expeditions all made with sanguine anticipation of finding and exploiting the great unknown continent. The results were uniformly disappointing, mere desolate snow-clad islands in latitudes which, had they been north of the equator, would at least have provided a temperate climate: Kerguelen Island, Marion Island, Crozet Islands, all valueless although within fifty degrees south of the line. But one deduction could at least be made from these efforts, that the French were hot on the scent, and that if there should be anything worth finding they were determined to find it. The

Spaniards from Peru sent expeditions which formally annexed Easter Island and Tahiti, although with no attempt at occupation. They also pushed up the west coast of North America, founded San Francisco in 1775–6, and discovered Nootka Sound in Vancouver Island, which was to be the occasion of another international crisis at a later date. In the 1770's the question of the Pacific was coming to a threatening head; and if the threat subsided and is now forgotten, that was the result of Cook's second great voyage, which was to prove that there was no southern continent to fight about.

Cook himself said that another voyage was needed to settle the question of the southern continent, and it was a foregone conclusion that he should be appointed to the command, "to put an end to all diversity of opinion about a matter so curious and important." He was now in the front rank of eminent seamen, although, in accordance with the time-lag of reward after service which is noticeable throughout his career, he was still only a lieutenant, a rank which other men were attaining merely for serving creditably as warrant officers. The King improved upon that when he summoned Cook to an interview in August 1771, and had him promoted to commander; but his achievement would have been more highly rated in our time. Shortly afterwards he set about preparations for the new voyage.

The Barrier Reef had provided illustrations of an avoidable risk, that of entrusting the lives of all concerned to a single ship. This time there were to be two, so that conceivably, if one were lost, the other might save her crew. There was of course no certainty about it, and in fact Cook's two ships were destined to part company fairly early in the voyage; while a later explorer, La Pérouse, had two ships, and both were lost with all hands by simultaneously striking an unknown reef. Cook was full of praise of the *Endeavour*. She was no longer in the first-class condition requisite, but two other Whitby colliers of her type were bought and fitted out regardless of expense. They were at first named the *Drake* and the *Ralegh*; but several people pointed out that this might hurt Spanish feelings, and by the King's direction they were accordingly renamed *Resolution* and *Adventure*. One wonders if any other government, French, Spanish, or American, would ever have renounced two proud national names out of polite regard for British susceptibilities. The *Resolution* was of 462 tons and the *Adventure* of 336, and they were nearly new at the time of purchase. In spite of this a sum greater than the purchase price was spent on fitting them for the voyage.

Joseph Banks was eager to accompany this second expedition, provided that he was to be allowed to have his own way on some important matters. These comprised the numbers of the

154

scientific staff and attendants, including two musicians, whom he wished to take with him, and the accommodation for their equipment and activities. For these purposes Banks used his influence with Lord Sandwich, the First Lord of the Admiralty, to get extensive alterations made to the *Resolution*. The ship's upper works were raised, a spar deck added, and a new cabin built above all. Cook disapproved, but wisely said little and allowed the facts to speak for themselves. They soon did. When ready for sea, the ship's draught was found to be seventeen feet instead of fifteen, a serious addition to a vessel that might have to be beached for repairs; and at the same time she had become so tender (or top-heavy) that she behaved in an alarming fashion while being worked down the Thames to the Nore. The Trinity House pilot in charge then declared that he would not risk his life and his character by taking her any farther, and one of the officers wrote to Banks to ask if he still wished to embark for the South Pole in her. The superstructures had been added on the orders of Lord Sandwich, who was not a seaman, and against the advice of Sir Hugh Palliser, Comptroller of the Navy, who was. Sir Hugh, always Cook's friend, now insisted that the alterations should be undone, and back went the *Resolution* to the dockyard to be restored to her original seaworthy state. In this business Cook's position was delicate, for Sandwich had always been his friend and patron, and it was invidious to take part in showing up a blunder from such a quarter. However, Cook chose his words well and got what he wanted without giving offence. Sandwich on his side was entirely untroubled by having wasted several hundred pounds from the public purse. It was indeed a mere fleabite compared with the total loss to the nation entailed by his methods of naval administration.

Banks, on inspecting the twice altered *Resolution*, was very disgusted and declined to proceed without accommodation proper to his designs. He asked that a frigate or an East Indiaman should be substituted for the collier. Cook could not agree, and Banks withdrew from the expedition. There was a temporary coolness, but it passed, and the two remained good friends. It was fortunate that Banks did not go, for a quarrel must have ensued. He had come to regard the shipping as transport for his expedition of naturalists and artists, while Cook's main object was geographical discovery.

As will be seen, the plan of the voyage involved greater hardships than those already experienced, and the fewer the landsmen the better it would be. The Admiralty engaged John Reinhold Forster, a German naturalist, to accompany the expedition; and with him went his son as his assistant. An artist, William Hodges, and an astronomer, William Wales, raised the *Resolution's* non-nautical complement to a modest four.

while William Bayly, another astronomer, sailed in the *Adventure*. When the expedition arrived at the Cape of Good Hope it found there a Swedish botanist, H. Sparrman, who was taken on the strength of the *Resolution* as an additional naturalist. The eminent scientist and nonconformist, Dr. Joseph Priestley, had been proposed as one of the astronomers and was willing to go. But the Board of Longitude, holding that a dissenter could not be relied upon for a trustworthy scientific report, vetoed the appointment.

The Board of Longitude was concerned in the matter because the function of the astronomers was to assist in making a thorough test of the chronometers which Cook was to carry for the first time. John Harrison, as has been mentioned, had won the prize which had been on offer for half a century. A duplicate of the prize-winning instrument, made by Larcum Kendall, was supplied to Cook, who had also on board the *Resolution* another chronometer independently designed and made by John Arnold. The *Adventure* carried two Arnold chronometers. Thus three of Arnold's instruments were to be tested against one of Harrison's.[1]

The instructions for the second voyage, in principle drafted by Cook himself, commanded him to settle the question of the southern continent. He was to sail to the Cape of Good Hope

[1] Gould's *Captain Cook*, pp. 91-2.

and thence southwards to rediscover Bouvet's Cape Circumcision, in about 54° S. If he could not find this land, or if, after finding it, the sea still appeared open, he was to go as far south as possible and then turn eastwards, circumnavigating the globe in the highest possible southern latitude. He was to explore and take formal possession of discoveries in the manner enjoined in the instructions for the previous voyage. He was to prosecute the far southern navigation only in the summer, retiring northwards for the winter into a more favourable climate. By this procedure Cook was certain to encounter any continental land-mass that might exist as far southwards as a ship could sail. It is to be noticed that the area to be covered was not solely that of the South Pacific, but of the Southern Ocean all round the globe. The intention was positively to find *Terra Australis Incognita* or to sail the seas that covered it. That national as well as scientific interests were involved was emphasized by the order that all officers and men after their return were to maintain secrecy about any discoveries that might have been made.

In the *Resolution* there were several of the former crew of the *Endeavour*, including those whom Cook had recommended for commissions, Lieutenants Clerke, Pickersgill, and Edgecumbe. In the written word Cook was never profuse either in praise or in blame, but he did record of the officers and warrant officers as a body: "I had all the reason in the world to be perfectly satisfied. . . . All of them on every occasion showed their zeal for the service in which they were employed during the whole voyage." The *Adventure* was commanded by Tobias Furneaux, who had been round the world with Wallis. By himself he would have ranked as an experienced and competent captain, but in comparison with Cook he was seen not to possess in the highest degree the qualities of a great leader: he showed always a little less drive and determination, a lower power of discipline, and a tendency to be satisfied with something short of the utmost performance. The crews of both ships were picked men. They were paid almost up to the date of sailing, and were equipped with an unusual outfit of warm clothing with which to face the icy South. Cook had all his anti-scorbutic precautions of the previous voyage. He was determined to make even more thorough use of them in order to prove once and for all that scurvy was an avoidable disease.

Cook sailed from Plymouth on July 13, 1772, in good time to begin the exploration by the opening of the southern summer. He stopped for supplies at Madeira and Porto Praya and reached Cape Town at the end of October. This preliminary passage served for shaking down and weeding out. The three Arnold chronometers proved so inaccurate as to be useless, while the Harrison went very well. By the end of the voyage it had established itself as the best means of finding longitude, better even than that of the lunars practised so successfully in the previous expedition. The first lieutenant of the *Adventure* became so ill that he had to be sent home from the Cape. The Forsters, father and son, revealed themselves as an incongruous element in the company. The elder Forster was a German of a recognized type. He was a competent man at his own job of natural history. He conceived that this gave him the right to pronounce judgment on everything else, including the seamanship and professional conduct of Cook and his officers. His judgments were always adverse. He handed them out in heavy censure, untempered by a ray of the imagination that enables one to put oneself in the other man's place. But he was not invulnerable in his self-esteem. He was sensitive to slights, quick to insist on his dignity, ready at all times to assert the importance of his position. Like so many Germans, he carried with him through life the callow puppyishness which the youth of other peoples shed as they grow up. His son was less prominent in the story of the voyage, but was by no means an amiable person. For the father it may be said that he suffered from rheumatism, had never made a long voyage before, and did not know what he was in for in going with Cook to the Antarctic.

Offended dignity raised a breeze before the expedition sailed. Forster was dissatisfied with the cabin allotted to him. He tried to buy the first lieutenant out of his with an offer of £100, which was refused. He then thought that the master's cabin would suit him; and since the master was a warrant officer and of inferior clay to the commissioned, Forster did not ask him but ordered him to exchange. On receiving the inevitable answer Forster became very extreme, declaring that he would report his adversary to the King and have him expelled from the Navy. The story got round, and for some days the sailors were heard gleefully making this threat to one another. And these flippant English were slack at their duty. The *Resolution* on one occasion got adrift from her moorings. It was Forster who noticed it and warned the officer of the watch, who was culpably inadvertent. Another time there was an outbreak of fire, very quickly put out; but the whole crew were adjudged to have been panic-stricken. On the passage south the two ships met some Spanish men-of-war, one of which, mistaking them for merchantmen and wishing to speak with them, fired a gun. Cook, knowing very well that his collier did not look like a King's ship, explained the position, and the incident terminated in civility. But Forster expatiated on his pusillanimity and the pitiable exhibition made by the masters of the sea. The worthy gentleman had indeed some ground for contempt of British politicians, if not of British seamen; for the government was paying him £4000 to make the voyage, equivalent to at least £10,000 now, and almost exactly the cost of the *Resolution*. In Frederick the Great's Prussia his value would have been drastically deflated.[1]

After refreshing his crews at the Cape, and hearing news of the French expeditions which had been working to the southward, Cook sailed towards the end of November in search of Bouvet's Cape Circumcision. He did not find it. Strong winds set him to the eastward, but he worked back to the longitude given by Bouvet and to a latitude several degrees south of his, without seeing land. It was thus clear that Bouvet's discovery could not be continental. It could be nothing more than an island, and perhaps nothing more than a mass of ice. Already Cook's ships had been encountering ice, from 50° southwards to the 60° which he had now reached at the beginning of January, 1773. It added to the hardship, and immeasurably to the danger, of the voyage; but the bergs yielded a compensation by providing an unlimited supply of fresh water in return for the arduous labour of hacking off lumps of ice and loading the ship's boats with it.

[1] Before sailing with Cook, Forster prepared the English translation (published 1772) of Bougainville's account of his voyage. The translator's preface is very much in the vein of the "patriotic Englishman" of the period, an amusing revelation of Forster's attitude before he had landed his big job.

A plentiful water supply was an important feature in the anti-scorbutic precautions, which now had to come fully into action. Signs of scurvy began to appear in both crews. Cook had one bad case, and Furneaux two, and there were a number of milder ones. All were treated with the fruit and vegetable extracts provided for the purpose, while the hygienic discipline of changing clothes, drying damp quarters by means of stoves, fumigating, scrubbing, and ventilating, was practised to the utmost that the weather permitted. The general result was that the sick recovered and the big threatened attack of scurvy was warded off. On the whole the health of the *Resolution's* crew continued better than that of the *Adventure's*, mainly because Furneaux was less exacting than Cook in making the men practise the somewhat unpopular precautions.

Failing to find Bouvet's land, and suspecting that it was insignificant or non-existent, Cook worked eastwards, according to his instructions, in the highest latitudes possible. In mid-January, 1773, he crossed the antarctic circle, the first time such a feat had been accomplished or even approached by any navigator since time began. These men were sailing the most completely unknown waters in the world, hundreds of miles south of the tracks of the latest French expeditions. They did not find the process agreeable. Gales and heavy seas, ice-coated decks and rigging, fog, bergs, and pack-ice in illimitable fields

formed the successive features of a four-months
programme. Yet, with scurvy averted, the ships'
companies throve, and the general health was
surprisingly good. Even Forster, whose recorded
opinions consist mainly of snarls and growls,
admitted this, although he was eloquent about
the sailors' sufferings. He was not much moved
by sympathy, except for his own share of the
discomfort, but he wrote of dangers and hardships with an underlying imputation against
Cook for incurring them. Already Mr. Forster
had had enough of the south.

Ice and weather forced Cook northwards again
after passing the antarctic circle, and he made
a search for the islands which, as he had heard
at Cape Town, the French had recently discovered. Their longitudes were uncertain, and
his course took him to the right latitude at a point
about midway between Kerguelen and the Crozet
Islands, neither of which he saw. All this time
Cook had been working eastwards while alternately increasing and diminishing his latitude.
In the vicinity of the French islands he was some
fifty degrees eastward of the meridian on which
he had first made 60° S. Having started the
search in the South Atlantic, he was now in the
southern Indian Ocean. He struck south-eastwards again and continued at 60° S. until he
was on the meridian of the western coast of
Australia. Continuing eastwards, he reached the
meridian of eastern Australia by the middle of

March. Cook had now fulfilled a substantial part of his instructions by sailing eastwards through 145 degrees of longitude (considerably more than one-third of the earth's circumference) at an average latitude of close on 60° S. In doing so, he had not sighted land, not even an island, much less the continent of so many ambitions. Some five of six degrees south of a section of Cook's track there lies indeed the coast of Antarctica, a windswept desert, unpeopled and barren, fringed by eternal ice and buried under eternal snow. Cook would have been glad to discover it and in fact suspected that it might be there. But it was not what he had come to seek, the *Terra Australis* of practical politics, with possibilities of new plantations and new articles of trade, capable of altering the balance of European sea power and national wealth. That *Terra Australis* was disproved for ever for the longitudes covered so far in his voyage, from the meridian of Greenwich to the meridian of Botany Bay.

The danger had been great, danger of crippling damage by the great winds and seas of the south, and danger of a sudden end by striking an iceberg in fog or darkness. The equinox was now approaching and the hours of darkness increasing, while the weather for the next six months would grow unendurably wild and cold. It was time to follow the instructions again and seek a milder latitude for the winter. Already the *Adventure* had parted company with the *Resolution*. Early in February they had separated in gale and fog in spite of the firing of guns and burning of flares. The rendezvous was a New Zealand anchorage. Captain Furneaux made straight for it, but Cook, as narrated above, carried on for five more weeks in the south, although the lack of a consort increased his risks. Not until March 16, 1773, did he turn north-eastwards for New Zealand, and nine days later he reached its coast at Dusky Bay with only one man seriously ill. At Dusky Bay Cook spent a fortnight on urgent refitting before going on to Queen Charlotte's Sound, the appointed rendezvous. There in mid-May he found the *Adventure*, which had been awaiting him for six weeks.

Furneaux had some bad cases of scurvy, and Cook's first care was to purify the blood of both crews by a liberal use of all the known precautions. He did not propose to spend the winter season in port, as Furneaux was making preparations to do. There was the question of Van Diemen's Land, whether insular or continental with New South Wales, to be settled. Furneaux had touched at Van Diemen's Land on his voyage to the rendezvous and had satisfied himself most erroneously that there was no strait between it and the land to the northward. His report persuaded Cook of the false interpretation and caused him to turn elsewhere. He decided that the winter work should consist in sailing east from New Zealand in latitudes higher than forty degrees and so traversing an unexplored tract that might contain a large mass of land. On the previous voyage, coming westward towards New Zealand, he had touched 40° but had made most of the passage in lower latitudes on account of the prevailing winds. These would be in his favour when going eastwards. Although this was not antarctic sailing, or anywhere near it, the undertaking was sufficiently arduous for a winter task. None of Cook's predecessors had come nearly as far south in this part of the Pacific. The result was negative, as Cook expected. Sailing with both ships on June 7, he kept between 41° and 46° S. until he nearly reached the meridian of Pitcairn Island, about midway between New Zealand and South America. Nothing whatever was seen but the empty ocean in six weeks' search. The health of the *Resolution's* crew was good, but the unfortunate *Adventure* was developing another outbreak of scurvy, which killed one man and determined Cook to turn northward for refreshment. He reached the Paumotus and thence turned west for the fruits and vegetables of Tahiti. The recorded facts allow no doubt that the difference in health between the two ships was due to the difference in command. The anti-scorbutic precautions were disliked by the men, and Furneaux's crew were neither compelled nor persuaded to use them with sufficient regularity.

The ships approached the southern side of Tahiti on July 16 and were in considerable danger from a cause that was frequent and unavoidable if any enterprise among Pacific islands was to be accomplished. The wind failed when they were close to a reef, and a strong current set them towards it. The answer was to let go the anchors and hope that they would hold. The *Resolution's* did not, and she bumped heavily until the tide turned and a breeze sprang up. Fortunately she escaped serious damage. The *Adventure* found good holding ground and did not touch the reef. In order to stamp out the scurvy Cook allowed six weeks in successive Tahitian anchorages, finishing at the original site of Fort Venus, where a camp was made on shore. The natives were pleased at his return and friendly in their manner. Yet all was not well, and the old care-free gaiety had gone. There had been dissensions and changes, and some of the dignitaries whom Cook and Banks had known were dead or had fallen to a low estate. A Spanish expedition had been to Tahiti since 1769, and a Spaniard was still on the island, lurking among the natives and not coming forward to make acquaintance with the English. A shadow, slight but presaging much that was to come, had fallen across Tahiti.

Leaving Tahiti at the beginning of September, Cook sailed westward through the Society Islands, where he was known and welcomed.

His purpose was to find further islands to the westward, of which the natives had told him and which he believed to comprise some visited by Tasman in 1643. This led him to the Friendly or Tonga group, containing Tasman's Amsterdam and Middelburg Islands. The islands were fertile and beautiful and the people pleasant, seeming to be as charmed with the English as the English were with all they saw. But the southern summer was now approaching, and with it the grim call of the Antarctic. Cook turned south for New Zealand, to make his final refit in Queen Charlotte's Sound and then to see what continents the far south might yield in Pacific longitudes. The course from Tonga lay along the eastern coast of the North Island, and here a prolonged and violent gale separated the two ships. After several days the *Resolution*, driven south of the entrance to Cook Strait, found a fair wind to return and duly entered Queen Charlotte's Sound. The *Adventure* was not there, and did not appear in the next three weeks. She had been driven farther to the eastward than her consort and had to beat back tediously against contrary winds. It was now November, and Cook was determined not to lose the season, even though he might have to sail alone. He left the Sound on the 25th, having buried written instructions for Furneaux at a well-marked spot. Four days later the *Adventure* came in, but the parting was final, and the

169

expedition forked thenceforward into two separate voyages. The loss of their consort did not depress Cook's crew, but had a lowering effect on Mr. Forster. He complained that every danger was doubled and vainly hoped that it might be made an excuse for shirking another plunge into the icy latitudes. But such were not the views of Cook and his officers.

They sailed the *Resolution* southwards from New Zealand to nearly 60°, and then south-eastwards to cross the antarctic circle again on approximately the meridian of Tahiti. The latter part of this push was through formidable dangers of floating ice, the cold was extreme, the sails and gear all frozen and very hard to handle, very little more warmth obtainable below decks than above. Yet the general health was good, and the crew continued in willing spirits. The unfortunate Forster was an exception. The bitter cold made his rheumatism worse, and the rheumatism made him more pessimistic and censorious than ever. There was no land and no sign of land. There might possibly be another New Zealand somewhere in the untraversed areas to the northward, but it could have no connexion with the antarctic cap. To avoid the thickening ice and relieve the extreme hardship, Cook turned generally northwards again, although always making way towards the west. Early in January, 1774, he was in the latitude of the southern end of New

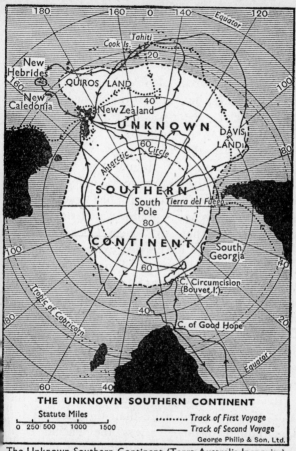

## THE UNKNOWN SOUTHERN CONTINENT

Statute Miles

0 250 500 1000 1500

.......... Track of First Voyage
——— Track of Second Voyage

George Philip & Son, Ltd.

The Unknown Southern Continent (Terra Australis Incognita)
as imagined in the Eighteenth Century
and
Its Demolition by Cook in the Course of his First
and Second Voyages

Zealand and about midway between it and South America. Still no land, no sign of land, no interruption in the great ocean swell, of a size and persistence possible only because no barrier existed for hundreds of miles. So far, over half the South Pacific, in latitudes never visited by man before, there was no continent, no large island, probably no small one.

After his northward breather Cook plunged south once more. On January 30 he attained the latitude of 71° S., more than four degrees within the antarctic circle. No one again reached this latitude for half a century, and no one has reached it in that area since Cook. He was stopped by a solid ice barrier, extending limitless on either hand. Behind it, if anywhere, lay the unknown continent, shrunk to a mere uninhabitable ice-cap. Cook made no claim to have determined whether it was or was not there. If it had been possible to go and see, he would have done so; but as it was impossible, he was not greatly grieved. The point was of interest to science but not to national policy.

In early February he was still south of the antarctic circle and more than three-fourths the longitudinal distance across the Pacific from New Zealand—on approximately the meridian of Mexico City. He had to complete the far southern circumnavigation by passing south of Cape Horn and skirting the South Atlantic until he crossed the track which he had made on quitting the Cape in 1772. There was enough of the summer left to do this, which would occupy some two months. But the ship and crew were strong, and the stores would last for a year. There was no continent, that was certain, but there was room for large islands to the north-ward of the waters which he had been searching. Cook decided that, having been sent out to explore, he would not go home while there was still exploration to be done. He would not make for the Cape and home in 1774, but would put in the rest of that year searching the still unknown areas of the South Pacific. Then in the season of 1774–5 he would round Cape Horn and complete the southern circumnavigation. He announced this decision and, says his journal, the officers heartily concurred, while the seamen rejoiced at the prospect of another year of this remarkable voyage in which the accustomed death-rate had become so completely inoperative. Cook was a man of penetration and a man who told the truth, but he may have been deceived about the sentiments of his crew. At any rate Forster says that they were painfully despondent (as undoubtedly he was) at the prospect of another year's southern cruising, and that they resigned themselves by degrees into a sullen indifference. Shortly afterwards Cook became dangerously ill with a bilious colic. His death would certainly have shortened the voyage, but all hands were unanimously grief-stricken at the prospect and joyful at his recovery. The witness to this is not his own journal, but one kept privately by a seaman. The doctor ordered the invalid fresh meat, which could be provided only by the slaughter of Mr. Forster's dog, the last living animal on board. It was converted into soup and, whether by coincidence or not, Cook was soon on his feet again.

Furneaux in the *Adventure* had reached Queen Charlotte's Sound shortly after Cook's departure. The buried message was found, and showed that Cook had left on a voyage which made it impracticable to fix a rendezvous. Furneaux had therefore to use his own initiative. He decided to complete the southern circumnavigation and make for the South Atlantic that season. While at the Sound he had a boat's crew massacred by the Maoris, not, it appeared, out of deliberate hostility, but in one of those sudden flare-ups that were always possible. He left New Zealand towards the end of December, 1773, kept a high latitude between 56° and 61°, and passed some 400 miles south of Cape Horn. He then crossed the South Atlantic and searched vainly for Bouvet's Cape Circumcision, after which he refitted at Cape Town and sailed for England. The *Adventure* reached Portsmouth on July 14, 1774. Furneaux therefore did not put in the extra year on which Cook had determined; but his passage south of the Horn was in unknown waters and, as it turned out, farther south than the track that was to be made by Cook in the following season. By arriving home before Cook he became the first commander to complete the circumnavigation of the globe in an easterly direction.

Cook's plan for 1774 was to sail northwards from his February position near the antarctic circle, and look for the eastern area of the great continent laid down by Dalrymple on the strength of vague Spanish reports. Part of this area had already been sailed over by Cook in his first voyage, and by Wallis, Carteret, and Bougainville, but its more northerly portion in 38° S. was yet untraversed. It was not large enough to contain a continent, but there might be islands. A group in this position, with a good harbour, might be a factor in Pacific sea power. After this there were other things to be investigated, the imperfectly located Easter Island of Roggeveen, and the large lands claimed by Quiros long before, a claim never yet satisfactorily cleared up. Altogether there was still plenty to do in the Pacific.

No land was found in the first-mentioned position, and Cook then tried for Easter Island, which he was lucky enough to find. It was a place of interest but no value, its anchorage and water supply poor, its soil not very fertile, and its natives already sophisticated by the visit of a Spanish ship from Peru. The great stone statues distributed about the island formed the chief interest and presented a mystery that has never been explained. They belong to a culture unknown in the historical Pacific and were certainly not made by the natives in possession in the eighteenth century. These were Polynesians of the general type, speaking a language like Tahitian. Specimens of the Easter Island statues are to be seen in the portico of the British Museum.

From Easter Island Cook sailed north-west into a tract north of the Paumotus. By so doing he came to the Marquesas, discovered by Mendaña in 1595 and never thereafter revisited. Their position was very ill recorded, and a close search was needed to locate them. Fresh provisions, including some extremely small pigs, were obtained, but trading was not easy, since the Marquesans were an isolated and contented people in whom it was difficult to stimulate wants. One "want," however, proved predominating, some red feathers obtained by one of the midshipmen at a previous port. Once they had seen these, the Marquesans would accept no other currency. And as there were no more feathers the economic intercourse broke down, and Cook sailed for Tahiti.

He arrived on April 22, 1774, having left in the previous September. He found the island changed for the better, with everyone cheerful and active, food supplies good, and himself almost deliriously welcomed. The *Resolution's* crew deserved some relaxation, and he stayed nearly a month. A Tahitian war fleet was being prepared in Matavai Bay for an expedition against another island. Assault exercises were carried out, the canoes entering from the open sea in line ahead through the gap in the reef, forming up in line abreast, charging full speed upon the beach, and discharging their warriors in a well-deployed force. This was merely training, and the expedition did not set out against the enemy while the English were there. Cook sailed in the middle of May, stopped at the Society Islands, and pushed westwards to pick up the tracks of Quiros.

Bougainville had already found and identified the island group of which Quiros had made a continent, but had not been able to stay long enough for accurate work. Cook made a more thorough investigation, naming the group the New Hebrides, fixing their position, and identifying the island and the bay which had been the scene of the mystic proceedings that had cost Quiros his command. The lofty islands set closely together might indeed be regarded by the eye of faith as continuous continent until the eye of science sorted them out and laid them down in a chart. Cook was not much enchanted with them or with their Melanesian inhabitants—to him a new and undesirable kind of South Sea islander.

All this occupied considerable time, and it was

not until the close of August that Cook was able to sail for New Zealand, to carry out the necessary refit in Queen Charlotte's Sound before going on for the third time into higher latitudes. On the way he sighted a large new island which he named New Caledonia. The landscape resembled that of New South Wales, and the natives were of a better sort than those of the New Hebrides. Wonderful to relate, they evinced no propensity to stealing and were in this respect unique among the South Sea islanders known to Cook. They did, however, purvey a poisonous fish, and casually remarked that it was not good to eat only after the English had eaten it and suffered thereby. Although the expedition spent ten days at New Caledonia, it was not enough for a proper survey, and Cook departed leaving half the coastline unexamined. Even then it took five weeks, until October 18, to reach the New Zealand anchorage. On the passage thither he discovered the Isle of Pines, surrounded by dangerous reefs, and Norfolk Island, uninhabited but capable of settlement, as the transporters of convicts in later days were to prove.

At Queen Charlotte's Sound the Maoris were friendly and glad to see him, although uneasy lest he should have heard of the killing of the boat's crew belonging to the *Adventure*. When they found that he had not, they gave him a very garbled account of the incident, making appear that the victims were from an unknown

178

ship having no connexion with him. Furneaux had found the letters buried by Cook, but had left none for him, and so Cook was in ignorance of the true story. He pressed forward his refit, and fortified his men for a long voyage by making them eat much wild celery and scurvy grass. On November 11, 1774, all was ready, and the *Resolution* sailed on the last section of her great voyage.

Cook's purpose was to reach latitude 54–55° S. and keep that parallel to Cape Horn. This would cross four of his own tracks [1] running roughly north and south on different meridians and would account for the unknown areas between them. After passing Cape Horn he would keep an east-going course between 55° and 60° S., and thereby skirt the South Atlantic, the last remaining refuge for *Terra Australis* in continental form, which, not being found there, would be found nowhere.

The *Resolution* sailed from New Zealand on November 10 and crossed the South Pacific without mishap, finding the seas and winds of the stormy latitudes in comparatively kindly mood. A week before Christmas the ship came in sight of the entrance of the Straits of Magellan. It was not Cook's purpose to pass through the Straits. As the weather was good he spent a fortnight in surveying the outer shores of Tierra del Fuego, on either side of Cape Horn. Of the

[1] One made in his first voyage and three in the second.

natives encountered he remarked that there was not a tall person among them. Between New Zealand and South America no land had been seen. It was certain that the South Pacific had no continental southern shore, and contained no islands of the largest sort. There was indeed room in the still untraversed areas for islands up to the size of New Zealand, although it would have been an unlikely chance that they should be so exactly placed as to be missed by the *Resolution's* tracks cutting all round them. It must be remembered that although the radius of visibility round the ship varied from thirty miles to nil, the presence of a great swell was a good indication that no large land existed for hundreds of miles in the direction from which it came. In fact no land large or small does exist in the part of the Pacific which verges towards the Antarctic.

After passing Cape Horn, Cook increased his latitude to cross the South Atlantic between 55° and 60°. A Spanish ship had sighted an island in the former latitude twenty years earlier, and Dalrymple with his continental proclivities, had embodied this ounce of fact in the ton of theory propagated by the sixteenth-century geographers. It was the last stronghold of theory. Cook duly sailed over his last continent and rediscovered the island, which he named South Georgia. Farther south and east, among the pack ice in 60°, he sighted another barren group of islands. The ice prevented near approach and he could not positively state that the southernmost was insular; so he named the discovery Sandwich Land, not Sandwich Islands. Thence he went north to the supposed latitude of Bouvet's Cape Circumcision, the search for which had begun the great exploration two years and a half before. Again it eluded him, but on February 23, 1775, he observed, with a certainty born of trust in the chronometer, that he had crossed his outward track of 1772. The circumnavigation of the southern world was finished.

He turned north and reached Cape Town a month later, having collected all private logs and journals and enjoined all hands to secrecy. After a month at the Cape he sailed for England, made an unhurried passage of three months with some scientific work on the way, and arrived at Portsmouth on July 29, 1775, just over three years after departing from Plymouth.

In the three years of hard and dangerous voyaging in all the zones of the earth's climates two great results had been achieved. The first may be very briefly stated, but is none the less important for that. It is that the *Resolution's* company of 112 had lost three men by accidental death and *one* by disease; and the disease was not scurvy. Cook claimed the fact as remarkable, but disclaimed any merit in achieving it, save that of "attention to my duty." He had, for the most part unconsciously, the faculty of writing a great deal in a few words; and what a volume of censure upon his predecessors that modest little statement unintentionally conveys. From Drake to Anson they had seen their men rot and die, and had not racked their brains to eradicate the curse. They had left it to a man of the eighteenth century, which was growing sceptical of many beliefs, among them that sickness was a visitation of God, to provide the remedy, attention to the neglected part of an officer's duty.

The second result was that the question of *Terra Australis Incognita*, almost as old as human thought, was settled. The southern continent positively did not exist in any latitudes short of 60° and, in places, short of the antarctic circle. Nowhere in the southern world were there hitherto unknown lands of any size, rich in natural products and peopled by advanced races having merchantable commodities to sell, lands in whose exploitation Great Britain would be obliged to take a leading part or forfeit her trading wealth and her sea power and her chances of retaining a great place among the nations. For, as has been noted earlier, to allow the French and the Spaniards to build up unchallenged a great mercantile sea power in the Pacific would have entailed ultimately the utmos peril to British interests in the Indian Ocean and the Atlantic; and would have made, ultimately the British Navy an inferior force to the navie of France and Spain. Cook's negative report set all this at rest. Although among ruling Englishmen there may have been some who were disappointed, the feeling of most must have been of relief. It was the summer of 1775, and the American colonies were ablaze. Troops, ships, and money had to meet the call; to what extent and for how long, none could tell. Spain and France looked on hopefully, with meditations of revenge for past defeat. A great new opportunity for mercantile empire-building could not have been sprung upon the sea powers at a worse juncture for Great Britain or a better for her rivals. Cook set the fear at rest.

There was indeed an antarctic land within the southern ice-ring. Cook himself was sure of it, although he had not seen it. The mighty bergs of the southern ocean were his evidence, bergs such as could not have been formed by freezing of the sea, but only by long-continued snowfall on hard land. This was the Antarctica of more modern exploration, but its purely scientific interest would not have moved the British government of the eighteenth century.

Cook's rewards were another interview with the King, promotion to post-captain, and appointment to a modestly paid sinecure at Greenwich Hospital; and, in another direction, election as a Fellow of the Royal Society on the score of his scientific success in the conquest of scurvy. For that achievement the Society also awarded him the Copley Gold Medal. He did not of course regard the Greenwich appointment as a title to idleness. It served to provide for his needs while he was at work on the account of the late voyage to be presented to the public.

Although the Admiralty had commanded secrecy before the search for *Terra Australis* had begun, and for that reason we have seen Cook impounding all the writings of his crew, the nature of the result made it unnecessary to keep anything back. The southern ocean held nothing to excite the mutual envy of the sea powers, the credit of having sent forth the expedition was humane and scientific, and the story could be freely told for the benefit of mankind. Cook was therefore to provide a relation of the voyage. He was dissatisfied with Hawkesworth's rendering of the material on the first voyage furnished by himself and Banks, and this time it was decided that he should be the author, with assistance from Canon John Douglas in seeing the work through the press.

First, however, there was trouble with Forster. He had always been resentful of Cook's inflexible pursuit of duty at the cost of danger and discomfort, and of his inaccessibility to advice to take easier courses. He had even written that Cook's success was undeserved, having been a rash gamble on good fortune. He now asserted that his £4000 was an inadequate payment and claimed that Lord Sandwich had promised him the writing of the account of the voyage and the profits of its sale. Sandwich denied any promise, most likely with truth. For, had such a promise been made, Forster, who was not a fool, would have obtained it in writing; and he had no such evidence to show. He had a fair claim to give the account of the results in natural science, and an arrangement was made that Cook should write of the voyage and the geographical discoveries, and Forster of his own department, the whole being revised for the press by Forster. Cook, without any of that assertion of his own dignity which might have been expected from a lesser man, modestly submitted to Forster's superior education, and handed him a good deal of manuscript for revision. Ultimately the arrangement broke down through a renewed disagreement between Forster and the Admiralty, and it was then decided that Cook should write with the assistance of Canon Douglas. But some time afterwards the Forsters published an unofficial story of the voyage, which they claimed to be drawn from their own observations, but which was detailed and accurate only in those parts on which they had seen Cook's manuscript, and vague and unconvincing for the rest.[1] An unpleasant pair these Forsters, who delighted in creating dissension. They set a story circulating to the effect that the failure

[1] Kitson's *Cook*, pp. 236–7.

of the Arnold chronometer on board the *Resolution* was due to sabotage by Wales, the astronomer.

Ultimately Cook's account was published after he had sailed on his third voyage. The book was a success, and the considerable profits were handed over to Mrs. Cook.

*Chapter Eight*

# The Third Voyage

AS noted at the beginning of this book, the Pacific presented to explorers two main categories of interest, the possibility of rich unknown lands, and the development of a trade-route or highway between Europe and Asia. After Cook's second voyage the latter interest remained. Already, it is true, there were two known routes across the Pacific from Europe to the Far East. One was by way of the Straits of Magellan or round Cape Horn. It had been used by Magellan and Drake and Cavendish and by some of the early Dutch expeditions, but experience had shown it to be too long and hazardous for regular eastern trade, which was better conducted by the Cape of Good Hope. The other was by way of Central America, involving transhipment and a land portage across the Isthmus of Panama or southern Mexico. The Spaniards operated this route by means of their plate fleets in the Atlantic and their Manila galleons in the Pacific, but the intervening land carriage rendered it suitable only for very valuable and non-bulky merchandise. There had been many British attempts to get a hold upon or a share in the operation of this route, from the Elizabethan designs upon Nombre de Dios and Panama to William Paterson's Darien Scheme of 1698 (part of the proposed operations of a Company of Scotland for Trade with Africa and the East and West Indies), followed by the right secured at the Treaty of Utrecht in 1713 for the South Sea Company to trade at Porto Bello, and later still by the capture of Porto Bello in 1739 and the despatch of Anson to the Pacific side of America in the following year. None of these operations had yielded any permanent success, and the Atlantic–Central-America–Pacific route remained, for what it was worth, a Spanish monopoly. Its worth was growing steadily smaller, for the nature of trade was changing. As the eighteenth century progressed, the cargoes from Asia became more bulky, and this was especially true of the China trade, where tea as the principal commodity superseded the gold, porcelain, silk, and lacquerware which had made the Manila galleons rather treasure-ships than ordinary merchantmen. The tea trade demanded an all-sea route without transhipment. It was being conducted between England and China by the Cape of Good Hope, the longest voyage frequented by British commerce. A route round the north of America, that is, the North West Passage, if it existed, would be much shorter and less vulnerable in time of war.

The problem of the North West Passage,

although not so old as that of *Terra Australis*, had had a fairly long life. The discovery had become desirable as soon as the emergence of America revealed that there was no clear run westward from Europe to Asia. The quest was pursued intermittently throughout the sixteenth century, and continuously for the first three decades of the seventeenth. These efforts discovered Davis Strait and Baffin Bay, Hudson Strait and Hudson Bay, and concluded in 1631, when the voyages of Luke Foxe and Thomas James (contemporaneous but mutually independent) put an end to existing hopes that a channel could be found leading to the Pacific out of Hudson Bay. From that time the search for the North West Passage was discontinued until the eighteenth century. Its revival by the British government in the reign of George III was due to a practical stimulus. The British Empire was changing shape. Its weight and emphasis were tending to shift from the Atlantic to the Indian Ocean and the Far East. The mainland American colonies were in an unsatisfactory state (their revolt, long foreshadowed, began in 1775), and their trade with Great Britain was not and never had been as important as that of the West Indian plantations. But the rich West Indies themselves had reached the limits of their value. The soil of the British islands was growing exhausted, while the French in Haiti and the Spaniards in Cuba were opening up new areas for sugar culture. More and more it was being recognized that the future expansion of British commerce must be in the East, with Clive's Indian conquests serving as an entrepôt and a place-of-arms for a vigorous expansion of enterprise into the archipelago and the China seas. The loss of the American colonies popularized this view, but it had been held by the initiated before the War of Independence began. It was for this reason that, within a year of his return from demolishing *Terra Australis*, Cook was out again to discover whether there was or was not a North West Passage.

Taking account of what was known at the time, we can conceive of the North West Passage as divided into two parts lying east and west of a central pool or lake in Hudson Bay. The eastern part from the Atlantic into the Bay was formed by Hudson Strait, well known and frequented by shipping for a century past. The western part, between Hudson Bay and the Pacific, was undiscovered and might not exist. It could not run out of the western or southern shores of the Bay and across to California in a comparatively genial climate. So much was known, because the Hudson's Bay Company had had its factors on those shores since 1670, and they could not have failed to detect such a channel. Moreover, one of its servants named Samuel Hearne had recently travelled on foot from the Bay inland, going westward and then northward until he came to the northern shore of America west of the Bay; and if there had been any channel to the Pacific he must inevitably have crossed it. It was certain therefore that there was no direct waterway south or west from Hudson Bay. On the other hand, it remained possible that a ship could sail northwards out of the Bay and then turn west for the Pacific, skirting the arctic shore of America which Hearne had reached at one point. It was a question that could not be settled by theory, but only by practical experiment. No one knew the lie of the land westwards from Hearne's point to Bering Strait, not even whether it was continental or a chain of islands or non-existent; and no one knew whether the available sea was permanently frozen or open in the summer, as Hudson Strait was open. The Admiralty planned an expedition for 1776 to go and clear up this problem, and to do so by approaching the unknown passage from its Pacific end.

There was no difficulty in finding a commander, although the Admiralty was at first unwilling to call upon Cook, conceiving that he had earned a spell of rest and leisure. That was not Cook's view. Already, before the new plan had been formed, he had been regretting that the future offered no prospect of active employment and contemplating without any pleasure the life of salaried idleness at Greenwich. In February 1776 he was asked for his advice on the new expedition, and Sandwich and other officials discussed the question of finding a man to lead it. He saw at once that the man must be himself and volunteered to go. To him it did not appear as self-sacrifice. He had no regret whatever at exchanging ease for hazard. Had he been such a man he would not have stood where he did.

There were again to be two ships, the *Resolution* of the previous voyage, and yet another Whitby collier, newly purchased and named the *Discovery*. She was the smallest of the four employed in Cook's voyages, just under 300 tons. The *Resolution* was fitted out at Deptford, and the work was very badly done, so that she gave constant trouble during the voyage; indeed it was in a sense the defects of the ship that led to the tragic death of her commander. The royal dockyards had a bad name throughout the eighteenth century, and at no time was it worse than under the administration of Lord Sandwich. Appointments were the reward of political support, and incompetence, neglect, and corruption were winked at. Cook himself remarked that in his exploring vessels the second-hand gear left over from their collier status would always last longer than the material supplied new from the dockyards. Throughout his ten years of exploration Cook expressed the greatest respect and gratitude to Sandwich, and the First Lord's support of Cook was undoubtedly disinterested and public-spirited. It is the brightest feature in an administration of the Navy which was not otherwise admirable.

The officers included some of South Sea experience. Charles Clerke, commissioned after the first voyage, commanded the *Discovery*. He was an able man of fine character. Unfortunately, before sailing in 1776 he was in debt through generosity to his brother and had to seek refuge from the money-lenders in the pestiferous Rules of the Fleet, a slum wherein debtors were free from arrest. Here he contracted the consumptive disease which was to shorten his life. Clerke's first lieutenant was James Burney, a midshipman in the previous voyage and destined to become an admiral and write the five-volume *History of Discoveries in the South Sea*. With Cook in the *Resolution* were lieutenants John Gore, whom we have seen in the first voyage, James King, and John Williamson, the latter turning out to be the only failure among those who served under Cook; and William Bligh, the master, destined in his pugnacious career to make a record voyage in an open boat after being cast out of his ship by mutineers, to earn Nelson's commendation at Copenhagen, and as Governor of New South Wales to be again overthrown by a mutiny.

Cook's instructions were to sail by the Cape of Good Hope to Tahiti, after looking for the French discoveries—Kerguelen and the rest—in the region south of the Cape. After returning to Tahiti or the Society Islands a native whom Furneaux had brought away, Cook was to cross the equator northwards and make for the west coast of North America in the region annexed by Drake and by him named New Albion in 45° N. He was to coast rapidly northwards, without stopping to investigate closely, to 65°, where he was to begin the search for the passage leading towards Hudson Bay, or towards Baffin Bay, the water between Greenland and America farther north. If the northern exploration was not completed in one season, Cook was to winter at a convenient place and try again next summer. Failing a North West Passage to the Atlantic, he might look for a North East Passage round Siberia and northern Russia to European waters. The instructions seemed to contemplate that the two seasons thus outlined would be those of 1777 and 1778. But there was very little chance for Cook, sailing in the summer of 1776, to reach the waters of Bering Strait less than a year afterwards; and in fact he did not reach them until 1778. Attempts had already been made to plant European vegetables and animals in the South Sea islands, and on this occasion the expedition carried so great a number of cattle, horses, sheep, and goats that Cook declared the *Resolution* to resemble Noah's Ark, lacking only "a few females of our own species."

The two ships made separate passages to Cape

Town, Cook in the *Resolution* sailing on July 12, 1776, and arriving on October 18 after calling at Teneriffe for wine by the way. Clerke, delayed by the pursuit of the money-lending fraternity, who were determined to arrest him although he was proceeding on important public service, did not sail with the *Discovery* until August 1, and reached the Cape on November 10. At the Cape there were two delays sufficient to preclude the fulfilment of the optimistic time-table of the instructions. The first was that the caulking of the seams of both ships had proved so defective on the voyage south that water continuously poured in through the decks and upper works. The men were wet in the living quarters, and the spare sails rotted in the sail-rooms. This was a specimen of the easy-going dockyard work already referred to, of which there was more to come, and Cook's crews had to re-caulk the decks and sides at Cape Town. The other delay was due to the Dutch bakers, from whom large supplies of bread had been ordered in anticipation, but who would not put the work in hand until they saw the ships in the anchorage.

On the last day of November Cook left Cape Town. He duly reached and examined the Marion and Crozet Islands and Kerguelen, finding them of no practical value. He then sailed on, diminishing the latitude a little, until he sighted Tasmania on January 24, 1777. He landed in order to obtain fodder for the animals and a tree from which to make a new spar, but did not investigate the question of Tasmania's insularity or continental connexion. On that head he was satisfied with Furneaux's report and wrote that it was established that Tasmania was the southern point of the continent. After a brief stay Cook departed for New Zealand, where he entered his familiar anchorage at Queen Charlotte's Sound on February 12. On the previous occasion the Maoris had told him their own version of the killing of the boat's crew from the *Adventure*. They now guessed that he would have learnt the full facts and were uneasy lest he should have come to take vengeance. Cook, however, realized that the affair had been unpremeditated, an affray arising from a petty offence between men who were sudden and quick in quarrel; and he decided to let it rest. The Maoris did not appreciate the civilized attitude. They had expected the English to exact blood for blood, and were contemptuous at being forgiven.

Cook sailed from New Zealand towards the end of Feburary. With a call at Tahiti obligatory, it was out of the question to be in Bering Strait by the opening of the arctic summer. There were therefore many months to be spent in the tropical Pacific before it would be time to sail for California and thence to the Arctic for the season of 1778. The voyage from New Zealand into the tropics was slowed by light winds and calms, and Cook grew anxious about the survival of the menagerie which he had brought so far. Not until March 29 did he sight a new island, one of a group which became known as the Cook Islands. At this place and at its neighbours there were no good anchorages, and intercourse with the natives was difficult, while no fodder could be obtained for the animals. This want was satisfied at the next group, the Palmerston Islands, where there were no inhabitants, but plenty of grass and fresh water. From here Cook turned westwards for the Friendly Islands, where the expedition spent a leisurely two months, increasing its knowledge of native life and customs, and hearing of important islands such as Fiji and Samoa, which awaited discovery. Cook did not proceed to these discoveries. He was hampered by the need to conserve the livestock, and the new discoveries of this voyage were to be in far distant regions. The ships were not in good state. They were leaking, particularly the *Resolution*, and had lost several spars.

At length in August Cook arrived at Tahiti and landed the animals, all in surprisingly good condition. They had been put on shore at the Cape of Good Hope, but otherwise had been over a year on board ship. Their bestowal upon the Tahitians was an act of benevolence on the part of George III, but to get them there must have cost his seamen something in unaccustomed stable work. A Spanish ship had been to the island since Cook's last visit and had landed a bull, but he was left a mere sideshow on the appearance of two saddle horses, upon which Cook and Clerke mounted and performed what they knew of *haut manége* to the admiration of all Tahiti. Omai, the Tahitian whom Furneaux had taken away, seemed not likely to settle down. He had behaved well and learnt much while in England, but among his own people his position as a man with tales to tell swelled his head and made him act foolishly. Cook accordingly took him on to his actual native place, Huahine in the Society Islands, and left him established with a house and a retinue and possessions which made him a rich man in native estimation.

With the close of the year it was time to sail for the north. In December the expedition set forward, and just before Christmas it crossed the equator. For the first time Cook was in the North Pacific, and for the last time he had left the South Pacific. The work he had done there was greater and more enduring than even he could know, and not least was the effect of that last year 1777, in which, more than ever before, understanding and respect were established between the English and the various islanders among whom the expedition had made prolonged sojourns. With different handling, the fate of the Polynesians might have been that of the

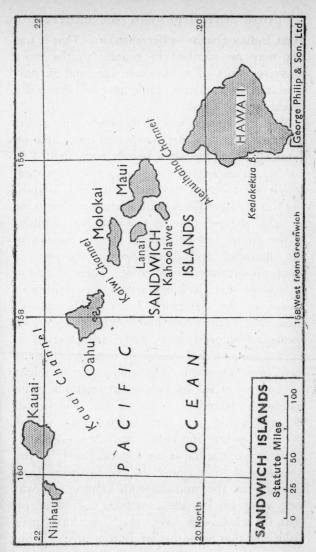

SANDWICH ISLANDS

Statute Miles

0  25  50  100

Kauai

Niihau

Kauai Channel

Oahu

Kaiwi Channel

Molokai

Lanai

Maui

Kahoolawe

Alenuihaha Channel

Kealakekua B.

HAWAII

SANDWICH ISLANDS

PACIFIC OCEAN

22

20

160

158

156

22

20 North

158 West from Greenwich

George Philip & Son, Ltd.

West Indian Caribs—extermination. That it was not may be ascribed in general to the more sensitive ethics of a humaner age, and in particular to the standards of tolerance and generosity established by Cook.

Now the voyage was of discovery once more. The first discovery, an unexpected one, came on January 18, 1778, when islands were sighted in 20° N., an important group as it soon appeared, which has received the name Sandwich Islands. On this occasion Cook, with a summer time-table to fulfil, stopped only at two outlying members of the group, but he realized the significance of the discovery and determined to complete it when opportunity should arise. There is reason to suppose that Cook was not the first European visitor to the Sandwich Islands. The natives themselves seem to have had traditions of previous contacts with white men, and Cook observed in their possession two pieces of iron, which must have been imported. The iron, however, might have been carried by Polynesian migrants. The Sandwich Islanders were of the widespread Polynesian race, and their language was similar to that spoken in Tahiti and New Zealand. More circumstantial is an historical story of the discovery of these islands by the Spaniard Juan Gaetano in the mid-sixteenth century. It was long accepted, but has now been discredited by critical scholarship. We may conclude provisionally that some earlier Europeans probably reached the Sandwich Islands, perhaps as ship-wrecked mariners [1] arriving in a boat; but that no one knows who they were or when the incident occurred. They left no record of the discovery, even if they ever returned to civilization. For practical purposes Cook was the discoverer.

He sailed away for the North American main-land on February 2, and sighted it on March 7. The point reached was about five degrees south of the present border between the United States and Canada. Bad weather prevented a rapid and at the same time close examination of the coast, while the general plan precluded any delay; for the real work of discovery was to be farther north. Cook therefore worked northwards at some distance from the land, and so missed seeing the opening of the strait between Vancouver Island and the mainland. He also coasted the outer side of Vancouver Island without realizing that it was an island. George Vancouver was serving with Cook in this voyage, but it was not on this occasion that his name was attached to the locality. He was destined to return some twelve years later in command of an expedition which made a detailed survey of the coast.

Penetrating the outer coast of Vancouver Island, not yet so named and still assumed to be

---

[1] Various possibilities can be thought of: Spaniards sailing on the Manila route; one of Cavendish's ships which parted com-pany in the Pacific in 1587 and was never heard of again; buccaneers of the late seventeenth century; privateers of the early eighteenth.

part of the mainland, Cook found a deep inlet which he called King George's Sound, but which was subsequently known as Nootka Sound. Some trade was done with the natives, a continental race very different from and less attractive than the Polynesians; and furs among other articles were obtained from them. These furs were in later years destined to play their part in a brief chapter of international trade and to assist in creating the Nootka Sound crisis of 1790. Spaniards had been up this coast as far as 54° N., and Nootka Sound was already known to them, but their explorations were unknown to the British. Cook stayed here through the greater part of April, the reason being the bad condition of his ships. Both were leaking, through ill-caulked seams, and the *Resolution's* masts were in need of repair and the rigging of renewal. On putting to sea again, the expedition met with very bad weather, and the *Resolution* leaked in new places to an alarming extent. Cook found a snug anchorage in which to heel the ship and expose the faulty seams, which were found to have retained scarcely any of their oakum caulking.

As far north as 60°, where he sighted Mount St. Elias, Cook made no real survey of the coast. Wherever seen, it presented the appearance of a continuous mountain range; and he must have been informed of Hearne's overland journey west and north-west of Hudson Bay, although

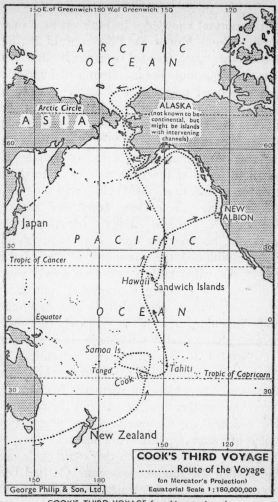

A R C T I C
O C E A N

Arctic Circle

A S I A

ALASKA
(not known to be
continental, but
might be islands
with intervening
channels).

60             60

Japan

NEW
ALBION

P A C I F I C

30             30

Tropic of Cancer

Hawaii   Sandwich Islands

0   Equator             0

O C E A N

Samoa Is.

Tonga       Tahiti   Tropic of Capricorn
Cook Is.

30             30

New Zealand

150      120

**COOK'S THIRD VOYAGE**
.......... Route of the Voyage
(on Mercator's Projection)
Equatorial Scale 1 : 180,000,000

150      180

George Philip & Son, Ltd.

COOK'S THIRD VOYAGE from his entry into the
PACIFIC to his death at HAWAII
*(The track in Bering Strait is simplified owing to
smallness of scale)*

that important knowledge had not yet been made public. From Mount St. Elias, one of Bering's points, the coast trended westwards, and here serious exploration began. Bering had recorded only disjointed points of land all the way to his passage round the continental tip of Asia. For all that was known with certainty, the solid main of America might end at Mount St. Elias and the rest be nothing but a string of islands. To put it in terms of the modern map, it might be possible to sail from the Pacific into the Arctic Ocean along the present borderline between Canadian Yukon and Alaska; and Alaska itself might be nothing but open water and islands. Cook established the continuity of the Alaskan coast. He sailed far up one deep sound which some on board thought promising, but it degenerated into a mere cleft in the mountains and, infallible sign of its nature, the water became almost fresh. Keeping fairly close touch, he rounded the south-western extremity, the Alaskan Peninsula, and passed through its continuation, the chain of Aleutian Islands. His direction was then northwards into Bering Strait. He reached its narrowest place, where forty miles of water separate America and Asia, on August 9. He was here on the arctic circle, and the best of the summer was gone. It had been necessary to spend this time in establishing that Bering Strait was the only approach to the northern sea, but the date allowed little hope that the work could be completed in one season. Cook determined to push on as far as possible before retiring south to winter quarters.

He followed the American shore northwards from Bering Strait until he came first into floating ice and finally against an impenetrable ice-wall in $70\frac{1}{2}°$ N., at a point which he called Icy Cape. After spending several days in a vain search for an opening in the ice, he turned west and tried the Asiatic shore, but could make very little progress beyond the narrowest part of Bering Strait. It was now evident that the season of 1778 was finished, and the ships headed south for an anchorage in the Aleutian Islands, there to do some refitting before sailing for the Sandwich Islands. On all the coasts adjacent to Bering Strait the natives, a Mongolian-Eskimo assortment, had obviously been in contact with Europeans. Some of them even raised their caps and bowed on meeting the English. At one place a letter was delivered to Cook, written in Russian and unreadable by anyone in the expedition. At length, on regaining the Aleutians, he fell in with Russian pioneers. They were fur-traders along the Alaskan coast and were very polite and helpful, particularly a much-travelled man named Ismaeloff, who had made the Cape of Good Hope passage from China to Europe. Not one of these men or of Cook's company could speak any language known to the other party. Communication was therefore restricted, which probably prevented Cook from learning new facts about the Alaskan coasts.

Sailing from the Aleutians, Cook took a month to reach the Sandwich Islands, of which he sighted a new member, Maui, on November 25. There was no anchorage, and he went on to Hawaii, a name which he rendered as Owhyhee, the largest island of the group. From November 30, 1778, to January 17, 1779, the expedition surveyed the coast of Hawaii without anchoring. On the last-mentioned date it found a good anchorage in Kealakekua Bay on the west side of the island. Cook was strongly impressed with the importance of the archipelago and evidently regarded it as in some respects the greatest of all his discoveries. He was not thinking of colonization, but rather of the Pacific highway and the strategic value of these islands half-way across and near the divide between the north-east trades and the variables farther north. During the passage south from Alaska and the examination of the Hawaiian coast the weather was rough and the *Resolution's* masts and gear gave constant trouble. One smash-up killed a man and injured three others, and Cook remarked that the cordage, canvas, and other stores issued to the Navy were not equal to those in use in the merchant service.

The ships had visited the western islands of the group a year before, and in recent weeks had been seen from the shores of Maui and Hawaii.

This encircling cruise caused great excitement among the Hawaiians, and gave time for a theory about the strangers to be developed and a welcome to be prepared for them when they should land. In Hawaii the priests were a strong element in society, stronger than in most of the Polynesian communities. The priests decided that the chief of the strange visitors in these unprecedented ships was one of their own gods, Lono, who conferred peace and happiness, and who had set out across the sea in time past, promising that one day he would return in a great ship. Captain Cook was Lono the god, who had gone away and had come back. It was a great religious occasion, and the priesthood took charge of the excited and mystified public. In innocence of all this Cook landed for the first time on the Hawaiian shore, to be mystified in his turn by the reception that awaited him.

All was ceremony and, as the English gradually began to suspect, adoration. Cook was clothed in a ceremonial robe, led in procession to a sacred enclosure, orated and chanted at, pressed to accept a sacrificial pig (too long dead) and coconut premasticated by the faithful according to ritual. He did not at first realize the drift of the proceedings and was uncertain to the end whether it was positively anything more than an embarrassingly friendly welcome to a strange chief. He did not therefore break out into hot denunciation of the blasphemous performance, as his missionary critics of later days considered he should have done. He had to remember his task of exploration and establishing friendly contacts with new peoples. His reception was at any rate cordial; and as a guest he owed civility to his hosts. When he had had as much of it as he could stand, he cut short the ceremonies without giving offence, distributed presents, and retired to his ship. Subsequent investigators who were able to question the natives of Hawaii became clear that what had taken place was worship of the god Lono and that Cook had been identified with the god. Cook knew nothing about Lono and did not understand the language in which the singing and preaching were conducted.

In religion on this plane there is always a non-spiritual element of material cost, which the public are expected to pay. The divine white chief and his semi-divine followers needed quantities of fresh provisions, and the priests enthusiastically saw to it that they were provided. The Hawaiians fulfilled their duty without overt grudging, but they held it to be an exceptional effort and were not prepared for the obligation to become permanent. There is a close historical parallel in the story of the Elizabethan pioneers in Virginia two hundred years before. First there was the exploring visit of Amadas and Barlow, who were mistaken for the immortal spirits of the dead returned to earth and were extravagantly welcomed by the Indians. Victuals, service, and adoring friendship were pressed upon them, and they departed to report that they had found a generous land with a loving and gentle folk. Next year followed the colonizing party sent out by Ralegh to settle. Neither the explorers nor the colonists had realized the religious basis of the Indian welcome, and among the Indians it quickly faded when the newcomers expected a permanent food contribution. Coldness, boycott, and war developed in succession, and within a few months the Indians and the white men were mortal enemies. Cook may not have read the Virginian story in the pages of Richard Hakluyt, but he was sufficiently experienced to be uneasy at the abnormal state of affairs in Hawaii and to be anxious to move on as soon as possible. Already the Polynesian propensity to thievishness was in evidence, and incidents began to occur from which ill feeling might arise. He determined to victual and refit and then to finish as far as possible the survey of the whole archipelago before going north again for the arctic summer.

The chiefs and the priests made a final levy of foodstuffs, and the people were no doubt resigned to doing the thing in style, since the thrilling but exhausting visit of divinity was coming to an end. Thus laden, the ships weighed anchor on February 4, 1779, and there was no intention of returning for that season at least.

Two days later the expedition ran into a gale in which the *Resolution,* almost as a matter of course in this voyage, received such injury to her foremast that it was necessary to seek anchorage at once to effect repairs. No anchorage had been found in the smaller islands and only one in Hawaii. To Kealakekua Bay the expedition, moved by the finger of fate, put back.

Among the natives there was consternation. They saw working parties coming ashore, astronomical instruments being landed, and the ship's mast hoisted out and brought to the beach. It was to be a stay of some duration, with more requirements of food. Where was this to end? The priests were on the side of the strangers, the chiefs divided, many of the common people mutinous. There was stone-throwing at a watering party and on February 13 a theft and pursuit which developed into a serious affray. A friendly chief was roughly treated in mistake, some of the sailors had a narrow escape with their lives, and the thief got away with his booty. Cook was perturbed. The white men had had the worst of the scuffle, and their prestige was lowered. He angrily remarked that this would not do and that he might be obliged to use violent measures. That night there was an offence of a greater magnitude. A large ship's boat was stolen from its moorings, and its whereabouts could not be traced. It was in fact broken up for the sake of the copper fastenings.

Next morning, the fourteenth of February, Cook determined to land with an armed party and bring on board the head chief as a hostage for the return of the stolen property. Someone said that the natives would probably fight, but he replied that they would not stand the fire of the muskets. By that he did not necessarily mean shooting to kill. He had often gained his point without real bloodshed, and he thought that the effect of firearms upon the Hawaiians would be all the more impressive since they had not yet seen them used. This proved to be a sad miscalculation.

Cook landed, with nine marines and their lieutenant, near the village on the western side of the bay. He went to the head chief's house and had a friendly conversation with him. The chief, an old man, was obviously innocent of the theft of the boat, and Cook meant him no harm. He invited him to come on board the *Resolution*. The old man was willing and they began to walk together to the waterside. Meanwhile an excited crowd had been assembling. Its members realized the offences of the previous twenty-four hours and understood that their chief, willingly or not, was being made a hostage. They were determined to prevent it. Some of them laid hands on him and forced him to sit down, about twenty-five yards from the water's edge. Cook saw no great danger, but Phillips, the lieutenant of marines, was convinced that there would be no getting away without a fight. He obtained Cook's leave to draw up his men in line with their backs to the water, in order to cover the captain's retreat when the time should come. Knowing nothing of firearms, the Hawaiians did not see the point of this and made no move to oppose it. Cook remained talking with the chief, while the bystanders grew more truculent. At that juncture a loud uproar arose at the back of the crowd. News had arrived that a canoe had been fired on by the English at the other side of the bay and a senior chief killed. At once the crowd grew dangerous. The men ran into the houses for their weapons and mat-armour, and the assemblage became one of three thousand furious, yelling savages. For a few moments Cook's gaze was a deterrent, and we may believe that it was his personality, not his divinity, that quelled the assailants. He gave up the attempt to take the head chief, and with the lieutenant, who had rejoined him, made his way slowly to the beach. It was only twenty-five yards, but difficult, for he could not turn his back.

An excited fellow rushed up and threatened Cook with an iron spike (a gift from the *Resolution*) and a heavy stone. He did not strike, but that would follow as soon as he had worked himself up to it. Cook judged that the moment for musketry had arrived. He carried a double-barrelled gun, one barrel loaded with shot, the other with a bullet. He fired the shot at the demonstrator. The charge must have been very weak, intentionally a mere frightener, for at short range the pellets did not penetrate the mat armour. Its wearer shouted with glee, and the moral effect was tremendous: the islander was proof against the weapon of the god. Then Phillips fired and was immediately knocked down. Cook fired his other barrel and killed a man, the marines fired all together, and the men in the off-lying boats were also firing. Contrary to all previous experience, the deterrent effect was nil. The Hawaiians rushed the musketeers, giving them no time to reload. All were now at the water's edge. Cook turned to call to the boats to stop firing and pull in. His cool gaze had alone held something down in the fury facing him. As he turned his head fury boiled over. He was struck down, half in the water, and butchered by a dozen men who fell over one another to get in their blow.

So, at the age of fifty, full of zest for the work awaiting him, died James Cook, the greatest explorer of his age, the greatest maritime explorer of his country in any age. These are not matters of exact computation; and if we cannot place Cook above Marco Polo, Magellan, and Livingstone, we are not forced to count him below them. He belonged to the great few. That it is safe to say. What he did and how he did it have been the subject of these few pages, short enough to need no summary. If they have conveyed an impression of a practical genius and a supreme craftsman at his task, they have achieved their object. If not, no last words will convey it.

It remains in this chapter to follow the expedition home after Cook's death, and in the next to survey briefly the age of Pacific development for which he opened the way.

Four of the marines were killed with him on the beach. Phillips, seriously hurt, and five others got away to the boats. There was dissatisfaction with the conduct of Williamson, the officer in command of the two boats. At least one modern biographer declares that he could have saved Cook and made no attempt to do so; but what his own comrades blamed him for was making no effort to recover Cook's body. The graver charge, it may be argued, breaks down on timing. The boats were lying off a short distance from the shore to avoid grounding. Up to the moment when the firing commenced Cook was in full command and bent on effecting a dignified withdrawal. He was quite able to call in the boats if he wanted them, and those in the boats had no greater reason than he had to believe that the situation was growing dangerous. The change came suddenly, and from the first shot to Cook's death it was a matter of seconds, a thing that takes longer to describe than it did to happen. After his warning shot failed to yield effect he ordered the marines to fire. They did so immediately, and the sig-

that not one of them fired twice.[1] In less than the time required to load a smooth-bore musket the party was rushed and Cook was down. How could the boats have saved him? On the other matter, failure to recover the body, there was indignation in the expedition. The fire from the boats did at length produce an impression, and most of the natives fled out of range. A resolute landing would have brought off the dead, but it was not attempted.

Cook's body was dismembered by the victorious natives and most of it burnt. The *Resolution's* mast and other gear were still ashore and had to be guarded until brought off. For a few days there were sporadic hostilities between the landing parties and the Hawaiians. Then among the latter a feeling of regret set in. They asked for peace and sent presents of foodstuffs, and finally, in a ceremonious procession, all that remained of Cook. Identification was made certain by a disfigurement of one of the hands, caused by an accident many years before. On February 22, the day of the funeral, all natives were required to withdraw from the bay, and the full ceremony of naval mourning was witnessed only by the white men as they buried their chief beneath the calm waters. As their blood cooled they

[1] Phillips fired twice, but he was reloading while his men were delivering their volley. It is hardly possible to give an incontrovertible account of the affair, since the statements of the witnesses are various and mutually inconsistent. Some of the narratives (e.g. that of Dr. Samwell of the *Resolution*) are by men who were not personally present at the tragedy.

sought no vengeance. The whole dis~~...~~ had been too evidently an accident of ungovernable excitement and failure of judgment. The Hawaiians on their side never lost their reverence for Cook, which continued to grow until the mid-nineteenth century. Then came a missionary who decided for professional reasons to eradicate it. He did so with success, collecting traditions from the old and ingeniously perverting them, and inculcating upon the young a version of the events of 1779, particularly of the adoration ceremony, which made the name of Cook anathema to the earnest, uncritical products of the mission school. Later still the islands were annexed by the United States, and it would seem that in respect of Cook the great republic was taught history by its small possession; for Americans in general are said to hold Cook in lower estimation than they should justly do.

Captain Charles Clerke succeeded to the command. He completed the refit and sailed north by way of Petropavlovsk to the Asiatic side of Bering Strait. The ice conditions of 1779 were worse than in the previous year, and the *Resolution*, which had wanted dockyard attention since the beginning of the voyage, was leaking badly. Clerke nearly reached but was unable to pass the limits previously attained. At the end of July he turned south, and a month later he died at the age of thirty-eight of the consumption which had first shown itself when he was evading the usurers. Captain John Gore, who had also served in all Cook's expeditions, and in Byron's and Wallis's before him, brought the ships home, touching at Canton by the way. Here the men sold at good profit the furs which they had gained from the natives of the American coast near Nootka Sound, a fact with considerable future importance. After a tedious voyage from China, lasting from January to October, 1780, the expedition at length arrived in the Thames after an absence of over four years.

## Chapter Nine

# · The Pacific Open

WITH the dissolution of the great southern continent the ambitions for economic empire building on the great scale south of the equator faded away. There was left the possibility of a modest but useful trade in the natural products of the countless tropical islands, and also the possibility of settlement colonies in Cook's New South Wales and New Zealand. But at the time the British home population was not spontaneously seeking an outlet by emigration, as it did in the nineteenth century, and it seemed that any colonies founded in the south would be of small size and due to some special incentive.

Interest in the North Pacific became greater after Cook's last voyage and especially after the treaties between Great Britain and the United States, France, Spain, and Holland in 1783–4, which closed the great struggle for maritime empire and American independence. As the result of that struggle Great Britain lost control over her original thirteen American colonies, but retained her hold upon Newfoundland, Nova Scotia, and the Canadian conquests made from the French. She retained also her plantations in the West Indies and her position as the paramount European power in India. In the Far East she strengthened her rights of navigation through the Dutch archipelago and increased her participation in one of the world's most promising lines of business, the growing tea trade at Canton. Tea was changing from a luxury to a necessity among some European populations, it was produced only in China, and it was legally shipped only from Canton. The demand was limitless. The difficulty was to find some means of paying for the supply. The Chinese would accept silver currency, of which there was not enough available, but they were not attracted by European merchandise. The Pacific was to produce more than one contribution to the problem of expanding the tea trade.

Cook had stayed some time at Nootka Sound in Vancouver Island. There the expedition had obtained a number of furs, notably those of the sea otter. During the visit to Canton on the way home it was found that the sea-otter pelts commanded a good market there. In the following decade the idea was developed. British merchants established a settlement of fur-traders in Nootka Sound, and the proceeds were shipped across the Pacific to play their part in buying tea in China. Before Cook's visit, a Spanish expedition had sailed up this coast and had discovered Nootka Sound. The Spaniards had made no settlement. They nevertheless denied the right of the British to settle, and in 1789 sent an armed expedition which forcibly removed the British pioneers. The news caused the Nootka Sound crisis of 1790. Spain justified her action on the principle of prescriptive right, the right to earmark without actually using any piece of unoccupied territory. In this case the prescription was connected with prior discovery, but it was not always so. Spain claimed a general prescriptive right to the whole Pacific Ocean, and on his last voyage Cook found an inscription implying Spanish annexation set up at Tahiti, which was undoubtedly a British discovery. Great Britain, then under the premiership of the younger Pitt, repudiated the doctrine of prescriptive right and asserted that of effective occupation. No matter who first discovered a territory, the right of possession was to the power which first occupied it by means of a permanent garrison or settlement. As in the Falklands dispute, Spain would have fought with the assistance of France; but France, preoccupied with the early stages of the Revolution, could do nothing. Spain gave way and restored Nootka Sound.

In this matter Pitt was not disputing over a trifle. He realized that the principle was of prime importance to the future of the British Empire, especially in the Pacific. Effective occupation as the title to new lands had been an English doctrine consistently enforced since colonization began. It was clearly enunciated in a charter granted by Henry VII in 1502, within a decade of the issue of the papal bulls of partition which were the first foundations of prescriptive right. Effective occupation is a principle that has not invariably favoured British expansion. It has given the French their title to Tahiti and New Caledonia, and the Americans theirs to Hawaii—all British discoveries which British governments were unready to follow up.

The Nootka Sound dispute made it desirable to clear up the geography of the American west coast, to which Cook had not been able to devote full attention. His intensive work had been on the Alaska coast, and he had not made a close survey of what is now British Columbia. George Vancouver was sent out to do this in 1791. He remained at the task until 1794, showing that Nootka Sound was an inlet into an island (Vancouver Island), charting the intervening strait, and giving final disproof, if any was needed, of the existence of any passage towards the Atlantic. Meanwhile Alexander Mackenzie, travelling by land, having discovered the Mackenzie River in 1789, leading to an outfall on the arctic shore of America west of the point reached by Samuel Hearne, made his way in 1793 across the Rocky Mountains to the Pacific coast north of Vancouver Island. The discoveries of Bering, Cook, Vancouver, Hearne, and Mackenzie established the shape and continental nature of north-western America and its Pacific coastline. An almost immediate consequence was the influx of British and American adventurers seeking trade-goods for disposal on the Asiatic side of the Pacific. They operated not only at Nootka Sound, but far and wide over a vast region that came to be called Oregon as the nineteenth century began.

The close of the War of American Independence in 1783 set in motion the train of events that led to the colonization of New South Wales. That name, it should be remembered, was applied by Cook to the whole of the east coast of Australia; and action soon to be taken by the British government was to define New South Wales as the entire eastern half of the Australian continent. Men of what may be called the old colonial habit of thought, those to whom plantations made more appeal than true colonies, had ideas of growing rich products in the tropical part of New South Wales by the use of Asiatic labour. Nothing came of it at the time, although Queensland, the part in question, has since become a plantation area. More immediate was the problem of the Loyalists, who had fought for the King in the American war and were now exiles from the new United States. It was proposed to settle them with governmental aid in New South Wales. They did not welcome the prospect, but preferred their own North America, and most of them went into the Maritime Provinces and Canada. Yet another post-war problem did lead to Australian action, that of transporting the numerous convicts produced by the low social standards of the eighteenth century. The convicts had hitherto been sent to the American colonies, and could be no longer. They were congesting the prisons and overflowing into the hulks of the old ships moored in the Thames, where they were kept in indefensible conditions. After much parliamentary discussion Pitt's government decided to send numbers of them to New South Wales.

Sir Joseph Banks recommended Botany Bay as the best pioneer site, although, as noted earlier in this book, he had not thought highly of it at the time of his personal visit some seventeen years before. Captain Arthur Phillip reached the Bay early in 1788 with an expedition comprising about 750 convicts, 350 soldiers and officials, and no free private settlers. Phillip immediately decided that the site was unsuitable and examined the great inlet farther north, which Cook had named Port Jackson but had not entered. On its shores the energetic Phillip founded Sydney within a week of arriving at Botany Bay. That location was abandoned and was never thereafter the headquarters of the penal settlement. It is curious that on the strength of one week's tenancy it should have become the symbol and byword of the whole system of

Australian transportation. To the popular mind, during the next half-century a conviction for serious crime meant going to Botany Bay, while in fact no convict after the first batch ever went there.

Only a minority of the convicts returned to England on the completion of their sentences, for the simple reason that no transport was provided to bring them home. The majority settled in New South Wales. So also did most of the time-expired soldiers of the garrison, one of whose officers, John Macarthur, laid the chief foundation of Australian prosperity by acclimatizing sheep. From the opening of the nineteenth century free settlers began to emigrate from Great Britain in increasing numbers. Very soon the numbers of free private individuals exceeded those of the prisoners and their guards, and with the stoppage of transportation in 1840 New South Wales quickly became a British community of the normal type. Meanwhile other colonies were taking shape: Victoria, Tasmania, and Queensland, offshoots or subsidiaries of New South Wales; Western Australia and South Australia, colonized by movements direct from England. There was in the early nineteenth century a period of social strain and material distress in the British Isles, and a widespread feeling among dissatisfied men that they could better their fortunes by pioneering overseas. That instinct created the dominions of the modern British

Commonwealth, with Australia and New Zealand prominent among them.

The New South Wales group of settlements were never purely continental in sentiment. They had always a maritime outlook and their ocean was the Pacific. One of their early interests was whaling, for whales were numerous in their coastal waters and all over the Pacific. Colonial whaling consisted of short passages in small vessels.

European whalers, having since the Middle Ages well-nigh exterminated the whale in the Atlantic, had followed him into the arctic waters round Greenland and Spitzbergen, but even there supplies were failing to keep pace with the demand for oil. Whalers therefore entered the South Pacific in force on the heels of Cook. While he was still exploring the north on his last voyage they were already numerous in the south. The whalers were mostly British and American (from the Atlantic ports, of course, for there was as yet no American Far West). At a later stage there were Frenchmen also in the trade. Pacific whaling entailed the longest voyages habitually made in all the record of the sea; for the whaler stayed out until he had a full cargo of oil, seldom less than three years, and sometimes more than five. Coupled with this, the hardship, discomfort, and danger were greater than in other sea services and the net pay very small; for as the years elapsed most of it was absorbed by purchase of clothes at high prices from the owners' slop-chest. Seamen of good character would therefore not sign on voluntarily for a whaling voyage, and most of the crews, apart from the nucleus of experts, were men who had been crimped or shanghaied or were dodging the law. This fact had a great influence on the future of the Pacific islands.

The whalers could not remain for years continuously at sea. They had to seek anchorage for victualling, watering, and refitting. They used the newly revealed islands of the Pacific from the Sandwich group north of the line to New Zealand far to the south. As individualists following no policy of state, the whaling captains had no scruple in paying for their supplies with cheap firearms and crude spirits. Their men also, tired of hardship, frequently deserted and went native, spending the rest of their lives in beachcombing idleness and not elevating the moral tone of Polynesia. Further than this, the whalers, being often short-handed, were given to taking off runaway convicts in the New South Wales ports; and these men played their part in disseminating vice and crime through the islands.

Similar effects were produced by some of the early Pacific traders. The eighteenth-century explorers who revealed the islands had not perceived the likelihood of any valuable trade with them. There were modest exceptions, as in New Zealand, where Cook noted the excellence of the pine timber and the Navy in subsequent years made regular visits for supplies of spars. But closer acquaintance showed more general possibilities, and Sydney and other Australian ports provided bases for exploiting them. The part played by Nootka Sound and the northern furs in the China tea trade has already been noticed. The tea trade was capable of further expansion if means of payment could be found, and before long the tropical islands were brought into its orbit. The Chinese market, indifferent to British manufactures, was eager for sandalwood, dried sea-slugs, and certain island birds' nests from which a stimulating soup was prepared. Soon after 1800, if not before, traders from Sydney were working the islands for these things, whose ultimate destination was Canton. Sandalwood was the most important, and remained so for fifty years. By that time the conditions of the China trade had altered, and the coconut products, copra and fibre for the use of European manufacturers, became the chief business of the island traders. An important branch of mercantile enterprise was the recruitment of native labour for the white men's plantations which were established at many places in the tropics, not only on the northern shores of New South Wales, but in islands such as the Fiji group where there were planters of cotton and sugar long before the annexation of the territory. Slaving under the British flag had been legally abolished in 1807, and the recruitment took the guise of indentured service for a term of years, with promise of payment and repatriation at its close. Sometimes these terms were honourably observed, but sometimes they were not. Ignorant *kanakas* [1] were tempted into indentures which they did not understand; and the departure of the active men upset the balance of small island communities, with disastrous social results. Recruiting or "blackbirding" was a sinister trade. Like others it was a phase which passed, first controlled then ended by the growing authority which nineteenth-century civilization was obliged to exert in the Pacific.

In the 1790's a movement began in England and Scotland which had an immense influence on the future of the Pacific islanders, the formation of a number of missionary societies. Of these, the London Missionary Society took the lead in the Pacific by sending missionaries to Tahiti in 1797. The British societies were Protestant, while a parallel Catholic movement took shape in France under Napoleon and became effective overseas after his downfall in 1815. The United States was also the home of a vigorous missionary activity, the Americans resembling the British in propagating a simple evangelical type of Protestantism. The social achievement

[1] The native pronunciation seems to be kánaka. Australian usage accentuates the second syllable, kanáka, with the vowel sound as in packer.

of the missionaries was of the first importance and may even have amounted in some places to the preservation of the native peoples from extermination. For the missionaries bridged the long interval between the intrusion of uncontrolled adventurers into the islands and the assumption of responsibility by civilized governments. In that interval a great deal of harm was done by the vendors of drink and muskets, the blackbirders, escaped criminals, deserters, and racketeers who preyed upon native simplicity; and the harm would have been infinitely greater but for the missionaries. Their activities were twofold, to report and denounce the ill-doers to European governments and clamour for remedial action, and at the same time to advise and fortify the island kings and chiefs and train them in the ways of civilized rule and negotiation.

In all this long period of over half a century (say from about 1800 to about 1870) the missionaries, with the exception of the French, were against European annexation, and were confident that the native rulers could be strengthened and educated to hold their own in civilized independence. The missionary success was never unquestionable, and in the end the policy broke down completely, so that in the last decades of the nineteenth century all the islands fell under the rule of outside powers. But in tiding over a phase of confusion a good work was achieved. It was also, of course, a lesser evil. The Tahitians,

Maoris, Hawaiians, were better off before they had ever seen a white man, and at best they were but rescued from some of the evil consequences. But the contact was inevitable from the day when Columbus sailed from Palos. There was a leaven in western Europe which had to penetrate the world.

On the American side of the Pacific the early nineteenth century witnessed change and enterprise and a general opening to the world's business. Spanish colonies occupied the whole coastline from the far south of Chile northwards to San Francisco. So long as the Spanish colonial administration remained effective no foreigners were allowed on this coast, and Spanish enterprise itself was restricted. The Napoleonic wars broke the system. British blockade severed the link between the colonies and Spain, and the *de facto* king was for years Napoleon's brother, whom all Spaniards loathed and whom the colonists felt justified in repudiating. The result was the practical independence of the colonies. When in 1815 the rightful Spanish king was restored the breach had become too wide to be closed. The colonies proclaimed themselves independent states. In some, like Peru, there were years of fighting. In others, like Mexico, there was very little. In all, independence was established, and Latin America took its modern shape. Spain did not lightly give up her hold. Bourbon France was inclined to help her, with a view to reward for herself; and absolutist Russia, reaching southwards from Alaska, seemed also likely to intervene. The United States and Great Britain warned off interference with the new republics, the first with her Monroe Doctrine, the second with her fleet. On the British side it was no new policy. For a hundred years past Great Britain had been anxious to see the Spanish empire independent and its trade open to all comers.

The new trade answered expectations, so far as the west coast was concerned. The silver mines were past their zenith, but new minerals were growing important, and guano, of which the arid sections of the Peruvian coast had a virtual monopoly, became a fertilizer of prime value to scientific agriculture. From about 1830 onwards for more than half a century guano was one of the most profitable of the new Pacific trades. Navigation on the Peruvian coast and the Gulf of Panama had always been hampered by lack of wind, and the region was peculiarly suitable for the introduction of steam shipping. The Pacific Steam Navigation Company of 1840, one of the earliest oceanic steamer lines, was an immediate success and did much to tighten the trading link between its headquarters in Liverpool and the South American Pacific.

The Pacific side of North America had important problems to be settled. Spain had already been obliged by Pitt to recede from her extreme claim to the whole Pacific coast. Meanwhile

American pioneers as well as British were penetrating the Oregon region. In 1819 Spain agreed by treaty with the United States to claim nothing north of 42° N. But Oregon was not yet formally either British or American, and the next challenge to their joint interest came from the Russians. They had been steadily extending their Alaskan sealing enterprise, and in 1821 the Czar claimed monopoly of the Pacific coast as far south as 51°. Americans and British both protested, and the Russian encroachment was one of the causes of the formulation of the American policy known as the Monroe Doctrine. In 1824–5 Russia reduced her claim by treaties with the United States and Great Britain, whereby the southern limit of Alaska on the coast was fixed at 54° 40′ N. This left Oregon defined as the region between the Rocky Mountains and the Pacific and between 42° and 54° 40′, but it did not settle the ownership as between the British and the Americans. Occupation was as yet sparse and the country remote from the regularly governed areas of Canada and the United States. For many years the question was designedly allowed to sleep while more urgent matters were tackled. Then the presidential election of 1844 brought it to the front. President Polk got in on an anti-British policy and a war-cry of "Fifty-four forty or fight!" That is to say, he claimed the whole of Oregon up to the Russian boundary. The extreme claim was dropped after the election, and in 1846 the Oregon Treaty effected a partition whereby the parallel of 49°, already the borderline east of the Rockies, was continued across Oregon. South of 49° was recognized United States territory, and north of it British, ultimately to be the province of British Columbia. The whole of Vancouver Island was also to be British. The importance of all these transactions on the long view was that Canada's prospect of extension to the Pacific was first imperilled and then secured. The fortunate outcome was emphasized when in 1867 the United States bought all Russian claims and became the possessor of Alaska.

The further diminution of Spanish North America on its Pacific side has now to be noticed. Mexico became independent shortly after the Spanish withdrawal to 42° N. had been made. Mexico was thus the successor to the rights of the old Spanish empire, and retained the coast of California and the port of San Francisco, afterwards to grow so great. But in 1845–6 war broke out on non-Pacific questions between Mexico and the United States. The Americans were victorious, and Mexico had to cede among other things the northern part of her Pacific coastline down to the present division between the two countries. Thus San Francisco and the greater part of California, full of Spanish place-names but not carrying a large Spanish population, fell to the United States.

The Asiatic side of the Pacific witnessed a period of vigorous opening to western enterprise after the days of Cook, although his work had only indirect connexion with it. The general settlement after the War of American Independence yielded to Great Britain the right of unimpeded navigation through the Dutch East Indies, and so facilitated the growth of the China trade. In the Napoleonic War this trade grew very important to industrial England, and vigorous measures were taken to defend it. One of these was the temporary British occupation of Java, whose capital Batavia was the chief seat of naval power in the Far East. Java was restored to the Dutch at the peace of 1814–15. But Sir Stamford Raffles, who had been its British governor, was impressed with the need for a British port in the bottleneck of trade routes between the Indian Ocean and the Pacific. In 1819 he acquired for this purpose Singapore at the extremity of the Malay Peninsula. At the time Singapore was an almost derelict fishing village. It speedily became a great seaport, a focus of trade routes, and a magnet for all the produce of the East. The secret lay in the policy enjoined by Raffles. The Dutch and the Asiatic powers of the Far East were all heavily restrictive of the business of any but their own people. Foreigners traded in their ports under tariffs, prohibitions, and oppressive regulations, intended to be discouraging. Singapore was from the first

234

a free port with a welcome for all. The East responded to the invitation, and trade poured in from all directions, as to an open market where the goods of all countries could be freely exchanged. Great Britain, then in the heyday of her industrial expansion, took first place in the free competition by virtue of the quality and value of her products. An instance is illuminating. China had hitherto shown no desire for European manufactures. But there was already in Malaya a considerable body of immigrant Chinese, who soon found that the British cottons available at Singapore were better and cheaper than those produced in the East. These people took to wearing British cotton garments and spread the fashion back to China, thereby helping to solve the problem of the hitherto one-sided tea trade. In general Singapore was a gateway to the Asiatic Pacific, where European intercourse developed from the trickle of the eighteenth century to the flood of the nineteenth.

At Canton the ships of all nations found their only legal access to China and its tea. In practice there was illegal trade with other ports, connived at by the officials for their private gain. The Manchu Empire of China was falling into decline as the nineteenth century set in, ceasing to produce able emperors and to inspire public spirit among their servants. At Canton the British trade was a monopoly of the East India Company until 1833, and was then thrown open. The private merchants who came into it lacked the diplomatic skill and deftness in appraising corruption which the Company's servants had acquired by long experience. Disputes and disquieting incidents grew commoner until they issued in the war of 1839–42 between Great Britain and China. Chinese law prohibited the importation of opium, and an enormous quantity of opium was nevertheless smuggled in. But it is entirely untrue to say that the British government fought to force opium into China. Palmerston, then Foreign Secretary, in a despatch to the British representative on the spot in 1839 denied any such intention; and when peace was dictated by the British three years later there was no alteration of the position of the opium traffic as illegal and disavowed. The smuggling could never have been developed but for the widespread corruption of Chinese officialdom. Before the war began the British superintendent at Canton collected two million pounds' worth of opium for destruction by the Chinese viceroy. The viceroy then demanded that the Chinese courts should inflict the death penalty on Englishmen charged with smuggling and other offences. This would have amounted in many cases to judicial murder, for Chinese law sent men to execution on evidence not regarded as sufficient by European standards. It was on this question of just and humane treatment that the war was fought. Its result was to open China to general trade. By the Treaty of Nanking Great Britain secured the cession of Hong Kong as a secure base of trade, and the opening of five "treaty ports." Other countries, France, Russia, and the United States among them, soon obtained similar privileges, and the number of treaty ports was increased in subsequent years. It was the beginning of the end of the imperial dynasty and the old Chinese civilization, the beginning of a century's disintegration with at length the promise of something better. But it had to be. The modern world (to record a fact without recording pleasure in it) has no room for hermits of any kind, least of all for hermit empires. We have all to follow the fashion.

Japan, another secluded country, which not only enacted but enforced non-intercourse with the outer world, was similarly opened by the United States. Dutch and Russian explorers in earlier times had gained an approximate knowledge of the coastline, but the Japanese refused contact except with a handful of Dutch merchants at one obscure place of trade. Nineteenth-century whalers desired to use the Japanese coasts for victualling and refitting, but were rejected. There was a blank area in the growing frequentation of the Pacific. It could not endure. By the middle of the century San Francisco had become a port of the United States, and there were plans for a steamer service between California and the newly opened China. It was a long passage for engines still in the experimental stage, and Japanese ports of call were essential. In 1853–4 two American naval squadrons visited Japan and enforced the opening of the country to trade, and, as in China, the other western powers soon shared the new facilities. The rapid westernization of Japan followed, with efficient armed forces and industries and a veneer of western civilization, leading to the bloodstained story of the rise and fall of Japan as a great Pacific power.

British interest in New Zealand was inevitable on more than one line of action. Before the eighteenth century was out Maori chiefs were paying visits to Sydney and learning something of British policy, strength, and intentions. White adventurers soon began to settle among the Maori tribesmen of the North Island. They were of the categories already described, deserters from ships, escaped convicts, traders, and land speculators. By 1840 there were reckoned to be about 2000 of them, British, American, and French, among a Maori population estimated at 100,000. They created great social disturbance, introducing firearms, drink, and European diseases, setting up extravagant claims to ownership of land, and keeping the country in continual ferment. Missionaries did what they could to preserve the peace, but could not claim much success. Their policy of standing as the power behind the throne and strengthening and purifying native rule was not applicable in New Zealand, where there was no paramount native sovereign but only a number of mutually independent tribes.

These circumstances created a whole generation of increasing anarchy in New Zealand. There was no law and order, and no hope that anyone in the country, Maori chiefs, missionaries or other white men, could create it. British action had produced the conditions, and the majority of the delinquents in New Zealand were British subjects. But the British government was unwilling to assume responsibility, and decades passed with nothing done and the scandals increasing. Then Gibbon Wakefield, one of the organizers of the emigration which was a feature of British life in the early nineteenth century, turned his attention to New Zealand. It appeared to be a very desirable country for settlement. He formed the New Zealand Company with influential support, and prepared to send out emigrants in large numbers to a country without a government, without any civil or criminal law, and without any defined and understood rules on the ownership of the soil. Similar plans were being made and companies formed in France, and it appeared unlikely that the British option to take the lead in New Zealand would remain open much longer.

The beginning of emigration forced the British government to act. Missionary influence was then very powerful in our home politics, and in deference to it the Colonial Office had held up Wakefield and his plans as long as possible. The missionaries would not have objected, in the case of New Zealand, to an annexation which produced good government and nothing more. But they did object to annexation coupled with an influx of white colonists; for they conceived that the unofficial European was the corrupting influence, the man who brought all their good work to naught. However, by 1839–40 it was evident that colonization in some form, French if not British, was about to take place and that no objections could stop it. The British government gave way and annexed New Zealand early in 1840, reluctantly taking charge of a situation which it could no longer refuse to face. This was the first annexation of Polynesian territory, exceptional because New Zealand was in a latitude and climate which attracted genuine settlers, as contrasted with the rootless adventurers who drifted through the tropical islands.

British reluctance to acquire distant possessions was not feigned and hypocritical as the traducers of the British name have so often declared, but was founded on solid and intelligible reasons. Until the middle of the nineteenth century the fighting vessels of the Navy were pure sailing ships, and for another thirty years after that, although they had engines, all their ocean passages were made under sail. In the transition period from sail to steam the engines were extravagant consumers of fuel, and coaling stations in the wide oceans were few and ill-supplied; thus the mechanical power had not the endurance for a long voyage and was limited to giving mobility in action. The result was that small, widely scattered possessions could not easily be covered by the Navy and formed a distracting liability. To defend them in war might cost the fleet more than they were worth, while to let them go involved loss of prestige and of bargaining counters at the peace conference. Inaccessible possessions similarly diminished the usefulness of the Army, the greater part of which was already split up in small garrisons posted all over the world, while the British Isles were dangerously ill defended. If Pacific islands were annexed they would sooner or later require garrisons—New Zealand called for troops after very short delay—and the Army would be still further dispersed in little stationary pockets of a few hundred men without chance of training above the parade-ground level. These, apart from the financial economy that appealed so strongly to the Parliaments of those lightly taxed days, were the grounds that made island-collecting distasteful to the men who were responsible for the strategy and administration of the Empire.

Tahiti was the first island on which such questions arose. The British missionaries who reached it in 1797 had ups and downs of fortune, but by 1815 had established their influence and the predominance of their faith. There followed a quarter of a century of the experiment which the benevolent were convinced would produce favourable results, namely, the preservation of native monarchy and independence, counselled by the missionary behind the throne, supplied by him with codes of law and rules for intercourse with outside powers, and civilized in its administration by the principles of gospel Christianity. In Tahiti the experiment was a success save in one indispensable factor, and in 1839 an American naval commander pronounced a handsome eulogy of the results. The exception to the missionaries' success was that they organized no national defence. Of course, they could not. Their work had been to put down tribal war and discourage the use of arms, and they lacked the will as well as the knowledge to equip their independent kingdom with an army strong enough to repel invaders. The defect was fatal.

Already in the 1820's the attitude of certain visitors to the island was alarming, and the Tahitians asked for the protection of Great Britain and the right to hoist the British flag. The request was refused by the British government for the reasons outlined above. In the following decade the threat became acute. French missionary priests arrived to establish Roman Catholicism in an island which had been Christianized by Protestants. The islanders did not want them and deported the first party.

They returned under cover of the guns of a French cruiser. Tahiti possessed not a gun of its own and could only submit. Once again, in 1838, Tahiti appealed to be accepted as a British protectorate, and again the request was refused. French ships-of-war haunted the island anchorages, and French priests multiplied on its soil. The outcome was the formation of a party to ask for French protection. It was not refused, and in 1842 Tahiti became substantially a French possession, although the puppet native sovereignty was continued and formal annexation was delayed until 1880. France, unlike Great Britain, was eager to acquire such possessions. To her they were no liability in war because, by her historical record, she was accustomed to the loss of distant colonies and her prestige was bound up with military campaigns in Europe. She took possession of the Marquesas at the same time as Tahiti, and in 1853 she annexed New Caledonia.

The Fiji Islands, although discovered by Tasman, lay off the track of the eighteenth-century explorers. Until proper charts had been made, their navigation was difficult and dangerous, and so they did not come into habitual contact with Europeans until the early nineteenth century, when traders began to visit them in search of sandalwood for the Chinese market. There followed the usual miscellany of deserters from ships, escaped convicts, collectors of trade goods, land speculators and planters, an un-

promising collection leavened by the presence of
missionaries with their policy of training the
native monarchy to its new responsibilities. In
Fiji it was a vain hope, and disorder steadily
increased for half a century. The Fijians were
more numerous than the Maoris of New Zealand,
although their islands were much smaller in area.
Lying well within the tropics, the Fiji group did
not attract true colonists as New Zealand did,
but was exploited by British, American, and
German planters who used native labour. The
complicated disputes on land titles, taxation, and
general civic liabilities, which were bound to
arise, and the utter inability of Polynesian chiefs
to cope with them, can be imagined. In 1858–9
the chiefs, under missionary influence, asked for
British annexation. A military expert advised
that the possession would be an embarrassment
in time of war, and the proposal was declined.
Ten years later things were worse, and a naval
officer reported on the ill doings of "the usual
class of lawless rowdies who congregate in these
places where no flag is flying and imagine they
can do just as they please with the natives."
Some flag had to fly, and at length, in 1874,
after protracted efforts to shirk the obligation,
the British government proclaimed annexation.

The Sandwich Islands may be taken as a third
example of the practical opening of the Pacific.
The fate of the whole group was always decided
by the proceedings at Hawaii, so much so that

a tendency has arisen to substitute that name for the group name bestowed by its discoverer. Cook's visits and death, and the subsequent calls of whalers and traders, had an unsettling effect on native society. By a political development the senior chief became more powerful and was recognized by foreigners as king. In 1794, already perplexed by foreign problems, he asked for British protection. A naval commander who was present took upon himself to hoist the flag, but the British government disavowed the act. Sympathy between British and Hawaiians continued, however, to be strong, although the conversion to Christianity was effected by American missionaries from 1820 onwards. The native kings, missionary trained, were better educated and more able than the generality of Polynesian sovereigns, but they were never really secure and successful. The French forced entry for their missionaries, and an uncomprehending British consul backed by an obstinate naval captain did his best to destroy the goodwill of Hawaii for the British; but the United States had as yet no desire to assume overseas responsibilities. The native population rapidly declined, while thousands of Chinese immigrants made up the deficiency. Although the titular monarchy continued, the administration was really in the hands of its unofficial American advisers. Hawaii in fact was an American dependency long before it was so acknowledged. In 1884, for example, the king's council consisted of twenty-eight Americans and six natives. Ten years later the monarchy gave place to a republic, and in 1898 American annexation was at length achieved.

The last-mentioned event has carried us far beyond the period by which the opening of the Pacific may be regarded as complete. That is best defined as the mid-nineteenth century, when China and Japan had been opened to general intercourse, British and Americans were well established in California and British Columbia, the United States had acquired San Francisco, Spanish America had become a series of independent republics, and the British dominions of the south had been founded. In the late nineteenth century Pacific questions were to enter a harsher phase with the intrusion of Germany and the American conquest of the Philippines from Spain, and in the twentieth an even more dangerous one with the tricky infiltrations of Japan.

# Authorities

BEAGLEHOLE, J. C., *The Exploration of the Pacific* (London), 1934.

CARRINGTON, HUGH, *Life of Captain Cook* (London), 1939.

CARRUTHERS, Sir JOSEPH, *Captain James Cook* (London), 1930.

GOULD, Lieut.-Commander R. T., *Captain Cook* (London), 1935.

HEAWOOD, EDWARD, *History of Geographical Discovery in the Seventeenth and Eighteenth Centuries* (Cambridge), 1912.

KITSON, ARTHUR, *Captain James Cook* (London), 1907.

MUIR, Surg. Rear-Admiral J. R., *Captain James Cook* (London), 1939.

WHARTON, Capt. W. J. L., *Captain Cook's Journal . . . made in H.M. Bark "Endeavour"* (London), 1893.

WOOD, G. ARNOLD, *The Discovery of Australia* (London), 1922.

Documents, plans, and photographs giving particulars of the *Endeavour* are to be found in *The Mariner's Mirror*, Vol. XIX, No. 3 (July, 1933), *H.M. Bark "Endeavour,"* by C. Knight.

# Index